Letters
from
Lillian

Published by the Assemblies of God
Division of Foreign Missions
1445 Boonville Avenue
Springfield, MO 65802

ACKNOWLEDGEMENTS

I Remember Mamma, adapted from the *Pentecostal Evangel,* May 14, 1972.

The letters in this book are excerpted directly from letters written by Lillian Trasher, though some of the letters have appeared in whole or in part in previously copyrighted periodicals published by the General Council of the Assemblies of God.

Cover art by Jim Burkholder

Contents

THE UNIVERSAL MOTHER

I saw the little children of the earth
Pass by me one by one —
I watched them idly, holding close the while
The hand of my small son.

My son was safe — he could not be a part
Of this strange throng that came
From everywhere — They were so hungry, cold,
So pitifully lame.

And some were crying, some had lost their way,
These children of the land;
I drew aside my skirts to let them pass,
And held my own child's hand.

I saw the little children of the earth
Pass by me in a line;
They blurred before my eyes — became one child,
And that one child was mine.

Then eagerly I ran to comfort him,
To feed and clothe him there,
To give him what his hungry heart had missed:
A mother's love and care.

And falling on my knees, I prayed, "Dear God,
Forgive, and let me be
Henceforth a mother to each needy child —
They all belong to me."

— Grace Noll Crowell

"I Remember Mamma"

Mamma had numerous titles such as "The Lady on a Donkey," referring to those early days in Assiout when she collected money by riding a donkey from village to village, and "The Great Virgin Mother of the Nile River Valley." But I think of her as the "Official Adopted Mother of the Assemblies of God." She is remembered all across America for her 51 years of devoted service to Egypt's children.

During the course of those years she reared more than 8,000 children, many of whom fill places of responsibility in government and the professional disciplines. In missionary circles when you mention Mamma, one person comes to mind: Lillian Trasher.

My wife Deborah and I served our first term on the mission field as Miss Lillian's assistants. As it turned out, we were the last appointed missionaries to be sent to the orphanage prior to her death. I've read her biographies and listened to the legendary stories of this great heart, but I'd like to tell you how I remember Mamma.

One of the first things you noticed about Mamma was her hands. When I met her, they were knotted and worn but something always stirred inside me when I saw them. The simple act of patting a little boy's head was like a benediction. Gentle hands.

Often she would join her "big girls" at the sewing machines. Mamma had a special place in her heart for these girls who never married. There is no way of knowing how many thousands of yards of cloth were cut by Mamma's large shears in making clothes for her "darlings." Strong hands.

As I made the rounds at midnight, it wasn't unusual to see her sitting at her desk writing to her hundreds of friends and financial supporters. She was finishing a 16-hour day that included everything from cuddling infants to settling squabbles. Tired hands.

No one stayed around very long without discovering that Mamma was protective. She possessed that fiercely loyal quality that characterizes all true mothers.

Once a man from a nearby village stole a part from the engine which generated our electrical power. Mamma was furious. She could never understand why anybody would take advantage of a single woman with so many children to care for.

I thought she might go straight to the village and make some fur fly, but not Mamma. Though still seething, she simply wrote a letter to the sheik of the village requesting his help in finding the "missing" part. She signed her name, then added a postscript: "We'll wait one hour before contacting the police."

Fifty-two minutes later the missing part was thrown over the wall. Everyone saved face, and someone learned that though Mamma was extremely generous, she most assuredly wasn't soft.

She looked at me, visibly relieved, and said, "Whew! For a minute I thought I had gone too far."

Ingrained very deeply in Mamma was the belief that if you kept anything for yourself, you were not living by faith. Mamma never bought a dress for herself in all her years in Egypt — she insisted that every penny go toward the needs of the children. The people of Assiout loved Mamma and con-

sidered her as their personal project and occasionally the
wealthy ladies would bring Mamma a nice dress. Invariably
they gave her a mock scolding. "Now, Lillian, don't cut that up
and make towels out of it." Mamma would protest such
goings-on, but she loved it.

When she sailed from America, young Lillian had no idea of
founding an orphanage. But the die of her life's work was cast
the night a dying mother handed Lillian a sick, filthy baby.

She prayed for guidance and the Holy Spirit led her to read
James 1:27: "Pure religion and undefiled before God and the
Father is this, to visit the fatherless and widows in their
affliction." Mamma lived by this principle from that moment
onward. As I worked with her in her last days, it was always
with the conviction that she had walked worthy of her calling.

As the orphanage family grew, more and more of Mamma's
time was consumed by her donkey trips. Finally she made a
deal with God, after reading Psalm 37:25: "I have been young,
and now am old; yet have I not seen the righteous forsaken,
nor his seed begging bread." She simply said, "Lord, You
furnish the bread, and I'll care for the children." Her theology
never failed.

Mamma was always grateful. I have seen poor peasant
tenant farmers humbly place dirty, crumpled-up *piastre* notes
in her hand and receive the same thanks that was accorded a
substantial gift from the landed gentry. Many people would
visit the orphanage to bring a gift and go away motivated to
live a more noble and beautiful life.

The orphanage was more than a humanitarian enterprise. It
was Mamma's way of witnessing. Not only were thousands of
children loved, educated, and provided for, but this was done
in a Christian context. This spoke eloquently of a com-
passionate Christ in a harsh, uncompromising, anti-Christian
society.

I shall always remember the visit by the minister of internal
affairs. All of the children stood at attention and saluted
smartly as the minister was presented. Mamma shook his

hand and said we were honored to have him visit. Suddenly, without a word, the children broke ranks and surrounded him, pressing in to touch him. They were dancing and shouting, "God bless you."

He was overcome with emotion at the sight of these hundreds of happy, well-cared-for children. His eyes brimmed with tears as he turned to Mamma and said, "For the first time in my life I have seen the power of God's love."

My fondest remembrance of Mamma was the day she came back from her last visit to America. The children had all been run through the showers and dressed in "church clothes." They lined the driveway and cheered as Mamma drove in. Mamma waved and cried — she had made it home.

When she got out of her car, the first thing she said was, "I was terribly ill in Detroit. I was afraid I was going to die over there. Oh, I'm so glad to be back with my children. It would have killed me to be buried in America." We all laughed, and she caught the slip.

Later she told Deborah and me to come into her apartment. When we entered, she grinned sheepishly and said, "I've got something in my suitcase." She opened it secretively, reached under all the clothes, and pulled out a case of steak knives.

She hurriedly explained that a lady in San Diego had given her some money on the condition that she buy something for herself. Mamma said that all her life she had wanted some genuine Sheffield steel steak knives. But the years of sacrifice were so much a part of her that she turned to me guiltily and asked, "It was all right to buy them, wasn't it, Dave?"

I hesitated a moment before answering. Mental pictures of Lillian Trasher's life flashed through my mind — the schools and dormitories built, the long hours of letter writing, the boils lanced, the lessons taught, the lives spared, the souls saved, the wars endured. I thought of the long shadow cast by this truly great mother, then I replied, "Mamma, I'm sure it's all right."

— David K. Irwin

Introduction

Letters from Lillian...a 51-year adventure! Perhaps you are a long-time friend and supporter of the Lillian Trasher Memorial Orphanage; if so, you will recognize in these pages the warmth and spirit Lillian Trasher gave to the orphanage she founded. And if you did not know her, I think you will begin to feel you do know her as her personality, beliefs, and great courage come to life in this collection of prayer letters she wrote to her supporters.

Except for a 1927 letter, we had no letters available that were written from 1911 — the year the orphanage was opened — to 1933. Possibly Mamma Lillian did not write many form letters during those early years, but rather wrote personal letters until the growing number of supporters necessitated sending duplicate letters. Adele Flower Dalton's article beginning on page 11 fills in the history of Mamma Lillian's youth and the early days of the orphanage.

The letters have been shortened to omit as much repetition as possible. However, certain themes — such as the frequent expansions to make room for more children — are seen throughout the book.

You will note the mention of various people who worked

alongside Mamma Lillian at the orphanage. While a number of these were appointed missionaries, of whom we have record, many lay people were also involved. Since it is not possible to name all of the people who deserve credit for their part in this ministry, we have not attempted to include a comprehensive list. In addition, thousands of people have supported the orphanage with prayer and financial gifts. To all of you, we simply say, "Thank you and God bless you." Your efforts of love in word, gift, or deed will not be forgotten by the One who keeps record.

Several books, including *Lady on a Donkey* (by Beth Prim Howell) and *Lillian Trasher: Nile Mother* (by Lester Sumrall), along with numerous booklets and articles, have been written about Lillian Trasher and the orphanage. We hope you will treasure this new book; it is a tribute to a great missionary and to the sacrifice and dedication that made possible this far-reaching ministry of the Assemblies of God.

— Beverly Graham, Editor,
and the Division of Foreign
Missions Editorial Staff

Part One:

Meet Lillian Trasher —
The Nile Mother

By ADELE FLOWER DALTON
Senior Editorial Assistant
Division of Foreign Missions

"Meeting Miss Trasher for the first time is an unforgettable experience," Christine Carmichael said after visiting the Assiout orphanage in 1946. "She is a large, lovable, gray-haired woman. Her eyes sparkle; her smile is infectious. She took pride in showing us her family. 'I now have 900,' she said. 'I don't see how I can take any more.' As she spoke there was a knock at her door. There stood a man holding a ragged bundle that held a tiny baby. It was dirty and had matted hair. One of Miss Trasher's helpers bathed the baby and dressed it in pink flannel. What a transformation! Once again the Nile Mother had opened her heart and another little life was saved."

Jerome Beatty, a world traveler and journalist, had given Lillian Trasher this title in an article he wrote for the June 1939 *American Magazine.* In it he declared: *Egypt is a land of wonders, but to me its greatest is Miss Lillian Trasher.*

Lillian's wedding was less than 2 weeks away that June day in 1910 when she sat listening to a missionary speaker. As she listened, the voice of God spoke to her 23-year-old heart with unmistakable clarity: *I want you to go to Africa.* Lillian's fiance, a fine young minister, had not heard this call. But Lillian could not deny it. She broke her engagement. With no promised support, except the assurance she was in the will of God, she made a reservation on a ship scheduled to sail for Egypt that fall. This was the African land where the Lord had shown her she was to go.

Lillian's older sister Jennie decided to go along to help her get settled in Egypt. As their sailing date approached Lillian wondered how God would supply her fare. But before that day arrived she had received every cent, much of it from people she did not know. Just before the ship sailed from New York, some friends prayed with the two sisters in their cabin. "Lillian," someone said, "ask God for a Scripture promise." When she opened her Bible her eyes fell on Acts 7:34: *I have seen, I have seen the affliction of my people which is in Egypt, and I have heard their groaning, and am come down to deliver them. And now come, I will send thee into Egypt.*

Lillian and Jennie reached Alexandria, Egypt, in October. They traveled to Cairo by train, then sailed up the River Nile to Assiout. "When I first saw Assiout," Lillian later said, "I thought it was the most beautiful place in the world." She joined a missionary family and began to study Arabic. On March 15, 1956, these words (speaking of Lillian) appeared on the front page of *El Ahram,* a well-known Egyptian newspaper: "She is a generous, respected lady who has labored for the good of our country for nearly half a century. She speaks our language in the sweet familiar accent of Upper Egypt."

From the day she arrived, it was the children, many of them ragged, dirty, and hungry, that gripped Lillian's heart. "I wanted to look after every neglected child I saw," she often remembered. About 3 months later Lillian visited a dying woman in a miserable hovel. Her eyes of love saw the woman's tiny baby girl. She heard her feeble cry as she tried to suck nourishment from a tin of milk that was stringy and green with age. When the mother died Lillian took the baby home.

All night long the baby cried. Disgusted, the other missionaries told Lillian to take her back. But Lillian knew that if she did, the baby would die. She went out, rented a small house for $12.50, then spent all she had left for a bit of furniture. That day, February 10, 1911, was the beginning of the Lillian Trasher Memorial Orphanage. Little by little other children were added. Lillian fed them, nursed them to health, and gave them what they needed most — love.

The small offerings Lillian received from her friends in America were insufficient to feed her growing family. Her first donation was 35 cents from an Egyptian telegraph boy. Other gifts followed, from Egyptians as well as from friends across the sea. "I believed that if God wanted an orphanage," she often said, "He would supply its needs. My family has never missed a meal."

Once, years later, when finances were very low Lillian explained to her children that she could not go into debt. They earnestly prayed that God would meet their need. The next morning Lillian received a check for $100. Another time when Lillian was away, the 4- and 5-year-olds told the cook they could no longer eat just lentils and asked for meat. "Darlings," the cook said, "I have no meat. You must ask God to give it to you." While these tots were praying in the nursery someone appeared at the door with half a beef. "My children," Lillian said, "are receiving lessons in faith."

In 1941, during World War II, the children needed both clothes and food, and there was no money to buy them. Lillian called the entire orphanage to prayer. Two days later she was summoned to Cairo by the American Minister to Egypt. He asked if she could use part of a Red Cross shipment of blankets, clothes, and food intended for Greece. Greece had been invaded and the ship bringing these gifts had docked at Alexandria. Prayer was answered!

"As a young woman," Lillian remembered in 1960, "I traveled through Egypt soliciting help. I went from village to village riding a donkey. Now I am 73, too old to ride donkeys. But as we pray God sends us what we need. Last year our expenditures were around $100,000, and there was some left over."

There were difficult times. The fifth child Lillian took was a 5-year-old boy who became desperately ill shortly after he arrived. To their horror, Lillian and Jennie discovered he had bubonic plague. Assiout's health inspectors dumped everything they had in tanks of disinfectant. Many of their possessions were ruined. Lillian became ill with a temperature of 105 degrees. After she recovered she was very weak. It was a discouraging time.

In 1947 a cholera epidemic claimed thousands of lives throughout Egypt. A newly-arrived boy, who had already slept in the nursery with 50 other children, began to have diarrhea and vomiting, then died. The orphanage was quarantined. But in answer to prayer no other child contracted this extremely contagious disease. One night before the quarantine lifted Lillian was wakened by the clanging of the school bell. The building where 40 small boys slept was in flames. The older boys had quickly rescued these boys. Then they pumped water and put out the flames. Once again, God intervened and no one was hurt.

Probably the worst time was in 1933. During a period of religious fervor all the children from Muslim families were taken away because Lillian was a Christian. Heartbroken, she watched more than 70 of her 700 children leave. "I am glad," Lillian later said, "that I did not run away when things were hard."

By 1916 Lillian had 50 children, far too many for her rented house. She acquired property across the River Nile, and moved into the first building before it was finished. Destitute widows came to help care for the children. As Lillian's family grew, other buildings were added. Classrooms were needed, also teachers. Lillian wrote and illustrated some of the text books and taught some of the classes. The boys who were slow to learn were given industrial training. The girls were taught domestic arts.

By 1923 Lillian was caring for 300 orphans and widows.

With so much loving care it was natural for them all to call her "Mamma." After her first visit Lillian's sister, Jennie Benton, returned often to Egypt. In 1948 Lillian said, "She is such a blessing. She knows Arabic quite well. She takes care of the housekeeping and teaches some of my classes. The children call her Auntie Jennie." Finally, Jennie Benton came to Egypt to stay.

For the first 16 years Lillian worked with and prayed for her children with little apparent results. Then in April of 1927 she wrote, "I have witnessed the greatest revival I have ever seen. Scores have been saved. Many have been filled with the Holy Spirit. I sent for the big boys who have left the orphanage and are living nearby. We prayed together and all 25 dedicated their lives to God."

During her 50 years in Egypt Lillian lived through various wars. In 1919 when her family numbered 100, an Arab uprising against the British created a reign of terror. Lillian called her children together to pray, then took them to an old brick kiln for safety. For three days bullets fell around the orphanage. The terrorists planned to kill Lillian and ransack the orphanage. But a neighboring farmer who was a Muslim protected the empty house. "For shame!" he told the marauders. "These are our own Egyptian children for whom this woman has given her life." Nearby houses were looted and burned, but the orphanage was untouched.

"I am sure," Lillian said, "the angel of the Lord encamped about us and protected us."

On July 1, 1952, during World War II word came that the Germans had entered Alexandria. All the other Americans left Assiout. When Lillian asked the Lord for a promise her Bible fell open at Exodus 14:13,14: "Fear ye not, stand still, and see the salvation of the Lord, which he will show to you today: for the Egyptians whom ye have seen today, ye shall see them again no more for ever. The Lord shall fight for you, and ye shall hold your peace." The German army never reached Assiout.

"What a marvel," Lillian Trasher rejoiced in 1960, "that out of the millions of Americans, God picked me. Oh, the joy of remembering the children and widows as they came, then seeing what God has done in their lives!"

Lillian kept the tiniest babies in her own crowded cottage. "My babies are my dearest possession," she declared. "Thank God we have never had to refuse any who needed us. If the Lord allowed me to live my life over, I would do the same thing for another 50, another 100 years. As much as I would like to go to heaven and be with Christ, I am not needed there. But these children need me very badly."

By 1961 1,400 children and widows were under Miss Trasher's care. But her health was failing. On December 17 a radiogram brought to America this sad message: *"Mamma Lillian died today.* Jennie Benton was with her sister to the end. "Poor Lillian," she said, "has been so sick these past 2 years. Now she is at rest."

As the gilded horse-drawn hearse carried Lillian Trasher's earthly remains through Assiout to the cemetery, people everywhere wept. In every window, every balcony the procession passed, people stood remembering this great woman who had loved so deeply and given so much.

During her 50 years in Egypt Lillian Trasher cared for more than 8,000 orphans. She is gone, but her ministry of love has not ended. Now, more than 20 years later, many hundreds of orphans and widows are still being cared for in what is presently known as the Lillian Trasher Memorial Orphanage in Assiout, Egypt.

Part Two:

The 1930s

April 7, 1927

Today I witnessed the greatest revival I have ever seen in my life. Three days ago we started a revival meeting among the children. The Spirit was with us from the very first meeting, dozens getting saved and dozens seeking the baptism of the Holy Spirit.

This afternoon I thought the children had better not have a night meeting; they had been praying and crying for hours, so I said that everyone was to go to bed early. I went to my room early also, but soon I heard such a noise coming from all sides that I sent a girl to see if a funeral was passing by. She returned and said it was the children praying everywhere. I went first to the widows' and blind girls' department and found they were crying and praying. I went to the big girls' room; they were all on their faces crying to God or shouting.

But the most wonderful sight I ever saw in my life was when I followed the noise up to the housetop. There were dozens and dozens of little girls shouting, crying, talking in tongues, rejoicing, preaching, singing — well, just everything you can think of — praising God! Several of the children saw visions. I have no idea of how many have been baptized in the Holy Spirit. Eternity alone will tell of these results.

It is as if a mighty fire has struck us. Nothing can stop it. It is as it was in the days of old when the Spirit of God fell upon the disciples. All school has been stopped. The children pray in the fields, on the canal banks, and in all the rooms. The house and grounds have become a "house of God." God is doing wonderful things with these little orphans.

I am now writing this a week later. The meetings are getting more wonderful. About 50 have been baptized in the Holy Ghost. Yesterday, I sent for all our big boys who have left the orphanage, who live or work near enough, to come. Most of them came and we had a special altar call for all the big boys. It seems almost too wonderful for words, but God saved every one of them! Then we had a dedication service and they all came up on the platform and dedicated their lives to God. There were 25 of them — some in college, some married, others ready to be married.

The revival struck the girls first, and all of the big girls were saved, then the widows, and now the boys! Oh, rejoice with me, rejoice with me! Can you imagine my joy? Seventeen years (and very dry years, too) of planting the seeds, then all at once to have such a wonderful harvest as this! If I had never seen the real results, I knew that the Word of God was being given to them day after day and year after year, and I knew it would spring up sometime, somewhere. But I never dreamed there could be a revival anywhere such as God has given us.

February 24, 1933

I wish to thank you very much indeed for your offering which was just received. Thank God for His faithfulness, and for His children at home who stand by us in these great days of testings.

You will be glad to hear that the Lord is giving us a revival and He has been working in a wonderful way in our midst. The need of more young men for Pentecostal work in Egypt is greatly felt these days when villages are calling for pastors and there are none.

Our older boys have never before shown such great interest in the Lord's work as they have this year. These boys are educated and capable, and of course the younger boys will follow as they are led by the older ones.

The mayor of a village nearby came and asked us to open a school and mission there, saying that he would deed us the land if we would build a room for the church and mission. We have decided to do it as there is no gospel work or school in that village, called Deir-Busra O, on the edge of the desert. One of our boys is going to preach and teach there full time.

Perhaps the work of all these years in the orphanage was to get such boys ready for the great work of taking the gospel to the dark villages. The joy of seeing my boys stand up and give out the gospel just fills me with joy.

In our afternoon meeting today in Deir-Busra O, one of my boys got up and preached for over a half hour. He is now a young man 20 years old. As I looked at him and heard the sermon that I shall not forget soon, I thought of those days when I took him in — a baby 4 months old. Seed planted years ago is just beginning to bring forth fruit.

March 13, 1933

Oh, it is wonderful how our loving Father uses His children thousands of miles away to meet the needs of little orphans day by day. We supply 2,100 meals a day and every day we start with nothing at all. But He always meets the needs.

The Lord has given us a wonderful revival during the past 6 weeks. He has worked especially among the older boys; many of them are going out as workers for Him in the villages near here. We hope to open several new schools and missions by September.

The orphanage lies in the center of a strip of land between the Nile River and the desert; this strip is called the Markez Abnube or Abnube County. It does not include the city of

Assiout; Assiout is on the west bank of the Nile and we are on the east bank. One can drive from one end of the strip to the other in about an hour. The Lord is burdening all of us for this county, that the villages may be won for the Lord. Of course we are the ones He expects to take them the light of the gospel.

One day a few weeks ago some of my boys and I were standing over the grave of one of our little girls who we had found dead in her bed, having been perfectly well the day before. One of the boys looked far across the valley and saw all of the villages, then he turned to me and said, "Mamma, God will require all of these villages of you."

I said, "No, son, not of me but of you boys; this is your work." He is the leader of this new village work now and I feel he will be greatly used of the Lord; his whole heart is in the work. Please pray for him.

I hope you will pray also for my sister Jennie Benton. Her home and all she had in the world was in Long Beach, California. An earthquake has destroyed everything. She is very sad, yet most thankful that she was in Egypt at the time and is safe.

Someone brought us tiny twin babies this morning. Poor little things — their mother died when they were born. They look very weak; I am afraid they will not live, but we will do our best. We now have eight little babies, ranging in age from a few days to several months. Then, of course, we have dozens of middle-sized babies, some just learning to walk. The others are known as the "big babies." How I wish you could have a look at them.

June 23, 1933

These are very hard days and it is only by the help of God that we are able to meet the daily needs of our large family.

I am very much in need of the prayers of all the Lord's children as there is a great stir among all of the Muslims against the missionaries here. This new feeling arose when a girl acted naughty and rude to one of the missionaries in the

Swedish Orphanage in Port Said. The missionary spanked her; she ran away and went to the police station, saying she been beaten because she refused to become a Christian.

This affair has stirred up all of Egypt; the missionary was sent out of the country at once! All of the girls who were Muslim were taken out of the orphanage and sent to a Muslim orphanage in Cairo.

This week's paper states, "A supreme committee of prominent Muslims has been appointed whose object will be to oppress the activities of the missionaries." While we were reading this report, a police officer walked in at the orphanage and asked if we had a girl named Pauline. I told him we did, and he said it had been reported to the governor that we had baptized this girl and had given her the name of Pauline.

Pauline is now about 22 years old. When she was a little girl she got lost in the desert, was found by an Egyptian soldier, and later was given over to the American hospital. When she was 6, she ran away from the hospital and came to me. I telephoned the hospital and told them, and they said I could keep her if I wanted to. So I did. When she grew older, Pauline wanted to become a Christian and be baptized.

I told the officials all of the story but they had something else against me. Pauline never got over longing to find her lost family, so more than a year ago she traced her mother and several younger brothers and sisters. Her father had died. The mother and brothers and sisters were very, very poor, so Pauline brought her little sister Miriam with her to the orphanage to be educated. But we did not baptize her.

We have many poor people on our charity list and Pauline asked if I would please put her mother down for $1.50 a month, which I did. Well, the report which went to the governor said that I was buying the girls to make them Christians and that the $1.50 was payment for them.

This all happened suddenly and it is an awful thing. The officials may take away all of our Muslim children and they may even send me home. Please pray for us.

July 20, 1933

For several weeks Egypt has been in a great stir; most of it is over the incident involving the Muslim girl and the missionary. The Muslims are making changes in order to hinder the influence of the Christians here, especially in the schools and orphanages. They have collected thousands of dollars to build new orphanages all over the country so the Muslim orphans will not have to go to Christian orphanages. Some churches have been broken into and the preachers badly beaten. Also, a convent was partly destroyed.

The governor sent several high officials to inspect every single thing in our orphanage. We had had many days of strain, wondering what the result of the officials' report would be. Of course I told them everything, keeping back nothing. I explained that the Muslim children went to all the Christian services just as the other children do. I told them how the Lord supplies our needs and about my call to work, and I gave them booklets and copies of our financial reports. After several hours here, they said they were delighted with the work but they were still going to build orphanages and take away the Muslim children from us. We have about 70 Muslims among our 700 children and widows. The head official asked if I would make him a present of a Bible, which of course I gladly did.

The governor sent for me and thanked me for all I had done for the poor children of Egypt, but he also said they were going to build orphanages and take care of the Muslim children.

Ten days passed and we heard nothing. I began to think they were not going to do anything. Then early one morning before breakfast, the same officials walked in. I was so frightened that I was trembling. I invited them in and asked if there was anything wrong.

They said, "No." I then asked if they had received a reply from the government. They said they had and they had been ordered to take all of the Muslim children at once.

Words cannot describe the sad sight as they took the children away. Pauline and Malazama remain with us since they are over 21 years of age. Pray that the teaching of years will go with these children and not die.

December 12, 1933

The cold days are here and the children are very much in need of more clothes. We thank God for the little extra money that has started coming in. We have been able to use it for sewing materials.

I have had over 2 months of illness with rheumatic fever, but I am now quite well again. I am sure that the Lord heard the prayers of the many friends who were praying for me. This illness was a wonderful lesson to me. Many times before I became ill, I would complain when I had to do work which I did not like. But now no matter how much I dislike doing a certain thing or no matter how tired I am, I thank God that He gives me the strength I need to do it. This illness was the best lesson I have ever had in life.

The situation in Egypt with the Muslims is much more quiet now; I do not think we will have any more trouble.

My sister returned to America in September. I certainly do miss her, but she had to see about her property. The people who are living in her houses will not pay the rent and she is depending on the rent money to pay her taxes.

I cannot tell you how very thankful I am for your help these hard days in Egypt. May the Lord bless you.

February 15, 1934

Can you imagine what it means for me to have the responsibility of seeing that 2,000 meals are provided daily as well as books, clothes, and the other needs for hundreds of children? This is a heavy job, even if one had all the money needed; it is impossible for us to have enough money for even one day in advance.

Also, these children come from so many different homes and have had little or no spiritual training or discipline. There are always many difficulties to settle. No matter how good the children are, if I only had to scold each child once every 2 years I would be correcting one child each day.

My mail is very heavy. I find it very hard to write in the daytime as I am interrupted so often, and I have a difficult time sitting up late at night to answer it. That's why form letters work well for me — they are much quicker and cheaper. A form letter can be left open and sent home for 2¢ while a personal letter, if closed, costs 10¢. And I can send my booklets and tracts in the open letter at the cost of 2¢. I sincerely hope you understand these reasons why I do not write you personal letters.

The Lord has been working wonderfully among the girls at the orphanage. Many have come to the Lord and are being baptized with the Spirit. Also, the older girls are beginning to be of much more help than in the past. It gives me great pleasure whenever I see them doing their part joyfully.

March 30, 1934

Sometimes as I look at the hundreds of bright little faces of the children sitting in church, my heart fills with joy when I remember that our Heavenly Father has chosen me to be the one to hand out both the Bread of Life and the daily bread for their little bodies.

A few days ago a rich man of the world, who knows nothing about trusting God, looked at me in utter surprise and said, "Do you mean to say that you have no food for tomorrow?"

I said, "No, we have none."

"Awful," said he. "Will you be able to sleep tonight?"

One of my friends laughed when she heard him say this. He turned to her and said, "It is no joke — she says she has no food for tomorrow!"

The young woman said, "Why, Lillian NEVER has food for tomorrow."

I told him that during the 23 years, the children had never missed a meal. "God has never failed," I said.

Today, as I am writing this, we haven't a cent. We have bread, but no food for dinner, no kerosene to cook with. The mail just came but there was no money in it. Yet we trust in the promise that our Father knows that we have need of all these things. May the Lord bless you for your great kindness and help to us.

October 20, 1934

I am very much behind with my mail and with all of my work these days. The work seems to get heavier every year, but I am so thankful that the Lord gives me the strength to go on day by day.

Miss Wespatat, our missionary (a trained nurse) who was in charge of the sick children, has been very ill with typhoid fever for about 2 months. One night the doctor told me she might pass away that night. I can never tell you how we all felt. Thank God she is better now, only still very weak.

The boys are still working hard at the different works which we have opened in the villages. I only hope the government does not do anything to stop the work. I heard today that the government had sent someone to take the names of all the boys in one of the schools. It may mean that they are going to try to hinder us. Even though things are quiet now, there is a very hard feeling against the missionaries.

One of my boys who I raised from a baby 6 months old is now a young man of 23 years of age. He has gone to assist Mr. Makiel Saleeb in the town of Souhag. Mr. Makiel used to be one of our teachers at the orphanage. About 6 years ago the Lord called him to open an orphanage in Souhag — a faith orphanage — and it is really wonderful how the Lord is blessing. He now has more than 70 children and a very nice building, and he is the only Egyptian who has a faith orphanage in all of Egypt.

Sometimes it takes a long time to see any results but God told us to plant and He would give the increase, so we go on planting and watering the young plants and someday the Lord will bring forth fruit.

P.S. I have just finished 24 years of missionary ministry here in Egypt.

December 13, 1934

I wish I felt stronger to begin the new year. There is so much I would like to do which I fear I am not strong enough to do. My heart is weak and I now have to be very careful.

The Bible tells us to bear one another's burdens; therefore, I want to ask you to join me in special prayer about the thing which is the greatest burden of my whole life. Since we started the plan of not buying anything which we do not have the money to pay for, I have suffered much under the strain of never having a day's food in advance. My request is this: that the Lord will send the money needed for our food at least a day in advance. I don't think anyone can imagine what a wonderful difference it would mean to me. I just cannot leave the children without a meal, and such a large amount of food takes a long time to prepare and cook. When no money comes in, I feel that I must go out and do what I can to collect it. Many say that I should have faith that it will come in without having to go out. True. Pray that I may have that kind of faith.

The girls have been making a lovely assortment of quilts from the scraps which we have left from their sewing of clothing. They love the beautiful American quilts better than any we can make here, but they are learning to make some very pretty patterns. Making quilts out of small pieces of material is a new idea in Egypt, and our married girls carry this idea with them to the different villages.

January 8, 1935

These are very busy days, but my larger boys and girls are more help to me now than they have ever been before. I have decided to teach one of my older boys to help me with my office work. Of course the boy will not be able to actually write the letters for me, but he will be able to make copies on the typewriter or duplicator, fold the letters and pamphlets, address envelopes and file new addresses. Such work takes hours of my time, and I think he will soon learn.

We are starting several new kinds of workshops at the orphanage including wicker chair construction and carpet making. We already have a good carpentry shop. We hope to take in a little money this way and at the same time teach the children the trades. Wages are very low in Egypt but foodstuff is cheap and plentiful and the poorer classes have learned how to live on very little.

The village people know nothing of games or amusements; their lives are hard work from morning until night. During the month of Ramadan the Muslims are not allowed to eat or drink a single thing all day long. They can eat during the night only. This observance varies a few days in the time it occurs each year. Sometimes it comes in the middle of summer. Those poor people work in great heat without a drop of water to drink all day long. The reason for this long fast is that their religious book, the Koran, teaches them that Muhammad fasted one day in the month of Ramadan. They are afraid that they will eat on a day that Muhammad fasted, so to avoid such an awful thing they fast the whole month! The women do not all fast and I have never seen them pray, but the men pray almost anywhere — on the streets or in any public place. They are not at all ashamed of their religion.

Women do not count for much with the Muslims. One of their beliefs is that the better a man is the more wives he will have in the next world! I have never heard what the reward of a woman is; no one seems to bother to try to find out. The Muslims are very difficult to reach with the gospel, but the Coptic Orthodox (the other main religious people of Egypt) are very glad to hear it. They believe in Christ but are in great darkness and need much teaching. Very few people in the villages know how to read the Bible. Much evangelism needs to be done in the small villages, but few are willing to sacrifice their comforts to go and live there.

March 18, 1935

These days we are trying to make enough new clothes for a family of 700; their old clothes are very old indeed! We have 60 girls sewing on the machines; each girl must sew one piece a day, pin her name on it and bring it to my office where there is a large chart or record of the girls' work. When a girl brings an article of clothing, she makes a cross opposite her name showing that she has done that day's sewing. Later, I look over each piece and if one is poorly sewn I send for the girl and have her do it over. These girls are on their own and are free to sew at any time that they can find a machine not in use.

Besides the sewing by these older girls, we have four classes of younger girls, 15 in each class. Each class has an older girl as an instructor and the girls sew by hand, each one working at a piece until it is finished. Twice a week the teacher brings me all the work which they have finished.

I do most of the cutting with the help of the older girls, and we try to make the time pass as pleasantly as we can. Someone gave us a lovely gramophone and some nice records with hymns such as "O, Why not Tonight," "We Are Going Down the Valley," "Onward, Christian Soldiers," "Joy to the World," "Silent Night," and several others. One of the girls puts the records on while we do the cutting. I am sure they will never forget these wonderful days — long after they have left the orphanage and have homes of their own.

The boys are doing well with the chair making; we are getting more orders than we are able to fill. School takes up most of the boys' time. The girls are also doing well with the carpet making, but it is rather a slow job. I think we will be able to sell more than we can make of these, also.

We had a very sad thing happen recently. One of our girls who has been married about 10 years and has four little children came back to us saying that her husband had gone blind and his family would not keep her or the children. Of course we took her in.

April 26, 1935

This year has been such a wonderful change compared to the last 2 years. Ever since I sent out the call for prayer I have not had to worry once where the day's food was coming from. Oh! It has made such a very great difference in everything. I now have so much more time for my home work. I do not have to go out in the heat as I used to have to do, and I feel so happy and thankful to see the children properly dressed and having their needs met. I just stop in the middle of my work and hold up my hands in thanks to God for the faithful way He cares for those who trust in Him.

Miss Wespatat, our missionary who was ill with typhoid fever so many months last year, has gone home to Germany. We hope that she will be able to return in October, but of course that will depend on how she feels at that time. Do pray, for she is such a great help to us.

The government is building a very large three-story building for the Muslim children, just a few hundred feet from our orphanage. The people of Assiout think it is a great shame for them to do such a thing but I do not mind much because most of their children are really my children, those whom they took away from us. Those little children call me on the telephone whenever there is no one around to hear them. One of the little girls was caught telephoning the other day, so I expect they will not be allowed the chance again. Some of the older boys come to visit whenever they can. They seem well treated but that is not what counts most.

July 26, 1935

Some time ago my sister built me a little cottage near our church. She also planted a lot of lovely fruit trees on the two-and-a-half acre plot. When I felt tired and needed a rest or change I used to come down here to spend the day, but I could not live here as the cottage is over two blocks away from the main building. As soon as I thought I was going to rest or sit down to a nice hot meal, a boy would come running up saying, "Mamma, you are wanted on the telephone."

A few months ago someone sent me a personal gift of several hundred dollars. I decided that one of the best things I could do with part of it would be to build a room onto the cottage where I could do the cutting of the children's clothes, do my letter writing, and put in a telephone. I then moved down to the little cottage. It is just lovely here, but I found that there was another drawback to the cottage — I was too far away from the small babies. So I started bringing them down here every afternoon and letting them play or sleep in the garden until sunset. A few weeks ago we took in a tiny baby 7 days old who had lost her mother. I decided to keep her with me in my cottage and feed her on goat's milk. This works very well with one baby, but since we get new babies all the time, I will not be able to keep more than one baby in such a small house. I have now decided to build a small cottage next to my cottage under some nice large shade trees, and keep all of the babies under 2 years old there.

We hope to start the making of the bricks for the new building at once. Our boys can make all of the doors and windows, which will cut down the cost. Anyway, I have money left from the personal gift I mentioned to buy the materials.

I feel sure that the babies will be much more healthy living in a cottage in the garden than upstairs among hundreds of other children. It will also be such a pleasure to me to see the little tots playing around in the garden like real "family" children, not like orphans.

August 30, 1935

You will be glad to hear that we have started working on the new cottage for the babies. Oh, it is wonderful how the Lord meets the needs as we step out on His promises. Lord Maclay, a gentleman who sent us a big donation last February, sent us $500 to help with the building!

The Lord meets our needs in such beautiful ways. A dear

sister who is a nurse in South Africa was once in Assiout. She makes $25 a month plus her board and room. She sends me $40 every 2 months and she has done this for about 6 years. Never has she missed sending the money, never has she sent less, and sometimes she sends more. She is getting old but she never worries what she will do when she is too old to work. She says that the Lord will provide.

I have another very dear friend who has sent me very large sums of money. He is alone in the world and lives on his pension from which he saves from his own needs and sends to the Lord's work. He is now over 93 years of age; last month he sent me $400. This is only one of many donations which he sends. Pray that God will strengthen his body.

A dear lady here in Assiout, an Egyptian, is bedridden, but the Lord has laid it on her heart to give treats to the children. When any new fruit comes in season, she sends $5, telling me to get fruit for the children — grapes, oranges, pomegranates, dates, sugarcane, watermelons, and cucumbers. Sometimes she will kill a fat calf and then give them a big dinner. When she was well she used to go around from house to house and give out food or money to the poor. Pray for her. She is unable to even turn over in her bed, yet she never complains.

October 26, 1935

About 2 weeks ago one of our older girls was to be operated on for gallstones. I had to rush out early to the hospital; the operation was to be at 8 a.m. As I was going out, one of our boys who is in charge of the meals said "Mamma, what is the orphanage to have for dinner?"

I said, "Fize, I haven't one cent and I am going to be late for the operation." I had gone about half a block when I noticed a man waving an umbrella. I wondered what was the matter. He came right up to me and took out his pocketbook and said, "Miss Lillian, someone who does not want his name known gave me this $50 for you."

I sent for Fize and told him to send the donkey cart to town and get all of the food needed.

After the operation was over the doctor came out and was talking to me about the needs of the hospital. I told him how God had provided the orphanage with the $50.

Later he was invited out to dinner at a friend's house and the subject of how God cares for His children was brought up. The doctor told them what the Lord had done for the orphanage that day. There was a rich young man there and as he heard the story the Lord put it on his heart to give the hospital $50. There was also another doctor present and the Lord told him to send for me and give me $50! The girl who was operated on is doing fine.

Last Sunday we had no money for bread. I went to visit a lady who had been ill. She said, "Oh, Lillian, I have been wanting to see you. I have $25 which I want you to use to buy a beef for the children's dinner and here is $25 more for any need of the orphanage." Just the week before the lady's sister had given me $25 for beef. (It takes that much for meat for one meal.)

The next day I was again without any money and we had no soap, sugar, or flour; our flour costs $560 a month. I went to see one of our girls off at the station who had just been married and was going to her new home. A strange man walked up and handed me an envelope with $25 in it and no letter. He refused to give his name.

I arrived in Egypt on October 26, 1910, 25 years ago this month. God has never failed me all these years; we are fed like the sparrows who have no barns or storerooms.

December 21, 1935

You will be glad to hear that we have moved into our new nursery. It is just lovely and we are all so thankful to God for it. There are two rooms which are not yet finished, but the workmen are doing their best to get them done as soon as possible. We have only moved the smallest children; those who are a little larger will have to wait a little longer.

I sometimes wonder if our friends wonder how we spend our days here in the orphanage, and what it is really like to have an orphanage in Egypt. School begins very early. Miss Clayton sees about the sick children before she starts classes at the Girls' School. The older boys have charge of the Boys' School.

I take some of the older girls who do not have to go to school and start cutting out clothes for the children. About half past 10 I go to town to get the needs of the day. I usually don't eat lunch before 2 o'clock, then there is the afternoon mail. If no money has come in for the bread for tomorrow, I have to go back to town and see what I can do about it. In some way God always meets the needs. After the food question has been settled, I have supper and start my mail.

Last night I sat up writing until a quarter past midnight, and as I got into bed I heard myself saying the very same words I had said the first thing that morning, "Oh, Father, I am so tired." But He gives me strength and I would not miss it all for anything! Such busy days make life so happy.

Some have asked me to tell them anything which I would like to have them pray about.

Pray that the older boys may feel a call to the Lord's work. Pray that the girls may take a greater interest in the house-work, and that the seeds which are being planted during my lifetime may go on growing until Jesus comes. Pray that the children will not only be Christian men and women, but that they will also take the Word of Life to others. Pray that the Lord will take out those who should not be in the home, and help us to never refuse any whom He would have us accept. Last year we all prayed that the needs would be met 24 hours in advance, and the prayer has been most wonderfully answered. I have had very little worry this whole year. Will you again join me that this condition may continue during the new year, that my time may be spent in things more important than seeing about food for the body.

March 4, 1936

One day, several years ago, I was giving out religious tracts and booklets about the orphanage work on one of the Nile tourist steamers which passes through Assiout. I walked up to a table where seven or eight ladies and gentlemen were having tea, held out one of my booklets, and said, "Would any of you be interested in reading about the Assiout Orphanage where there are about 700 children?" A young man spoke up and said, "No, I would not." Then one of the ladies said, "Oh, I would like very much to see one of your booklets."

I went and sat at some distance while the lady looked at the pictures. She got up and came over to where I was and handed me $5. That same evening she came to the orphanage about 8 o'clock. As she entered she said, "Miss Trasher, this is my father, Lord Maclay." I showed them over the place and they were very pleased indeed. As he went out he handed me $100. After that he sent me money every Christmas, sometimes $50, sometimes $100, and sometimes $250.

Last month on February 15 I received a wireless message from Lord Maclay, who was on a steamer at the time, asking me to meet him in Cairo February 17. Since he was returning to Scotland on the same steamer he would not have time to visit Assiout.

When I went to meet him in Cairo he was most interested in all that I told him and in the many photographs which I had with me. He asked me if there was anything that I was especially in need of. I told him that the children were badly in need of clothes. He said, "Well, Miss Trasher, I am going to give you $5,000." It almost took my breath away. Oh, the clothes, the cows, and the food that I could now buy! He then told me that I was to take a certain part, which he named, for my own use. How I thanked God for answering my prayer.

His daughter came in from a walk while we were yet talking, and said, "Father, it was I who found Miss Trasher!"

I said, "Found me? I am sure that I am no 'find'!"

He looked at me most seriously and said, "Miss Trasher, you have no idea what it has meant to me seeing your work. I went back to Scotland and opened a home for tiny infants after I saw all of your little babies and we now have 30 babies in the home." He is a trustee in the orphan homes of Scotland where they have about 1,200 children. They had never accepted infants before. I was so thrilled to think of those 30 little Scotch babies having a home just because he had seen my work. Praise God for His wonderful ways, which are past understanding.

March 20, 1936

Some of my dear faithful friends have often wished that there was something more that they could do to help me. I am wondering if we could not form a sort of prayer fellowship. You could ask your friends to join in this fellowship. I will tell you the needs and you can put this idea before the Lord and your friends.

1. Pray that the older boys will be called to the Lord's work.
2. Pray that one or two of our own girls will feel the call of leadership among the other girls. This is a very great need; no missionary will do for this special work. The leader must be someone who knows the language and who will live among the other girls.
3. Pray that the Lord will enable me to pay the salaries when they come due.
4. With such a big family there are many trying circumstances to be faced every day. Pray that I may be given wisdom and justice, that God will direct me in the decisions I have to make.
5. Pray that I may have the health and strength to do all that I have to do. Summer will soon be here, and I am very tired and nervous these days under the strain.

A short time ago I was invited to tea at the home of one of the Presbyterian missionaries. We lacked 50¢ having enough for the flour and we had no cooking butter or oil. While I was drinking my cup of tea, I looked up to the Lord and prayed. I remembered how we can hear people talking over the radio from Europe and America. Then I thought, *As we hear the radio, so God and the angels can hear all we say, so surely it has been heard in heaven that there is no butter and no cooking oil in the orphanage.* I rested on that and went home.

One of the older girls came in and said, "Mamma, did you get enough for the flour?"

I said, "Nearly enough." Then she laughed and jumped up and down and put $10 in my hand, saying, "A strange man who did not give his name came and gave this to me for the orphanage."

I then told her of how I had felt about the way our prayers are heard not only by God himself but by all the angels, just as we hear the radio messages. I slept that night with a strange peace, not because of the $10, but because I felt that those in heaven care about the orphanage butter.

May 27, 1936

For many months we were all sad to see that there was no spirit of revival among the children. It was becoming a great burden to all of us as there seemed to be a spirit of carelessness and a great lack of spiritual interest. You can imagine how discouraging this has been to us who have given our lives, not just to feed and clothe the children, but to lead them and others to Christ. We had reached the place where something had to be done, but what? Any change must come from the heart and the heart cannot be forced.

I was more upset about the girls than I was about the boys. I felt led to have a special meeting in the church one night. Not feeling too well, I took a chair, sat on the platform, and told them how brokenhearted I was over their spiritual condition. I was so broken that I could hardly talk. The Lord was with us. The girls saw their condition and began to weep and cry. Oh, it was a wonderful sight. Some of the worst behaving girls rushed up to the altar, grabbed my hand, and asked for pardon.

Some screamed out to the Lord for mercy. There was not a dry eye in the church. I cannot describe what it was like when we all got down to pray. Oh, how I thanked the Lord for His blessings, and for His care of all of our needs both spiritual and temporal.

Still the boys and the widows needed a refreshing. A few days after the Lord touched the girls, our pastor came to me and said, "There is going to be a three-day revival in the Pentecostal church in town. May the girls go?"

I said, "No, it is too far for the girls to go at night and if they all went the church would not hold half of our girls. Ask the ministers who are holding the meetings to come and have some meetings with us here in the orphanage. Then everyone can attend."

Well, they came and the time was ripe. The Lord started working with everyone — boys, girls, women, and all. Last night the meeting went on for hours. One of the older girls refused to leave the church until she prayed through to God. At last we had to tell her to go to the girl's building so things could be closed for the night. She went and the girls started a meeting in the middle of the night. The boys did the same thing and this morning I could hear the songs of joy from the boys' buildings.

The little boys, without anyone knowing, sent a list of their names to the minister (Pastor Saleb of Alexandria Church) saying that they wished to form a Prayer Army like the one which they have in the Alexandria church.

As I was leaving the church last night, one of the most difficult girls I have came up to me and said, "Mamma, I am going to start a Prayer Army among the girls and I shall put my name the very first on the list."

June 22, 1936

You will be glad to hear that the revival has now been going on for several weeks and many are getting through to God. The meetings have been held mostly in the afternoon, but several of the little boys like to spend a large part of the day praying in the church. Prayers and songs can be heard in the dormitories until nearly midnight. There is such a great change in the spirit of everyone on the place.

Some of you prayer partners have asked that I tell you when the special prayer requests have been answered.

(No. 1) I had asked prayer that some of the boys be called to the Lord's work. Just last week one of our brightest boys, a boy about 18 who is now in high school, sent me the following letter. (Don't forget that English is not his first language. That is why he has worded it so strangely.)

Dear Mamma:

I am so pleased to tell you that I have a great desire to serve God in the future. I am from this instant between the hands of God and the hands of yours. Please, Mamma, do your best to prepare me for God. Indeed, I do not deserve to be in His service, but may He bless me and strengthen me, not for anything but that which I can do in His Name. Many, many thanks. Your very obediently son, Ibrahim Hanna.

(No. 2) I requested that one of the girls be called as a leader of the girls. This has not yet been answered.

(No. 3) I requested that the salaries would be paid when they were due. This has been answered every month since the request has been made.

(No. 4) I asked that the money for the food would come in a few hours before time for preparation of the meals. This has been answered every day since the request has been made. Continue to pray.

July 27, 1936

I am enclosing a little booklet of pictures which will give you a better idea of the work we are doing than if I were to write a long letter trying to describe it. Hundreds more children have been changed just as these have, but I neglected to take a photograph of them when they entered the orphanage.

It gives me great pleasure to be able to help these little children along the rough pathway of life and make things easier for them. I feel sure that the next generation will be very different because all of those who have passed through our doors will know how to train and educate their children in the ways of the Lord.

My work reminds me of a fable of a little boy who was crossing the desert alone. He became very thirsty so he was obliged to dig in the ground with bleeding fingers until he came to water. He drank and went on his weary way.

Each time he became thirsty he dug holes and his hands became more torn and bleeding. At last he reached the other side, exhausted and fainting, his clothes hanging in dusty rags.

Some months later he looked across the desert and saw a happy little boy coming with his hands full of fresh flowers. The child was coming the very same way which he had traveled. He looked at the strange sight in perfect amazement. When the little boy arrived, he asked him how it could be that he had crossed the awful desert and looked so fresh and cool. The child answered, saying, "Oh, the way is beautiful. There are many small wells out of which spring lovely, cool water, and around each of these wells there are flowers and shady bushes and soft green grass. I had no trouble at all in crossing!"

The first boy looked down at his own scarred fingers and knew that it was his suffering which had made the desert bloom and had made the way easy for other little boys to cross. But no one would ever know to thank him or to ask who had dug the wells, but he knew and was satisfied.

As I think of this lovely little fable, it gives me courage to go on digging holes in the desert that my girls and boys may be able to face life with the help of God and a knowledge of Him, as well as with a strong healthy body and a brain that has had a chance to develop.

The years have not all been "digging holes." There have been bright, beautiful days of love and joy as well as the days of heavy burdens. There are always some who come back with thankful hearts and make me forget the dark days and hot nights.

October 24, 1936

Day before yesterday I was reading the story of the feeding of the 5,000 and I was very much struck by these words, "And Jesus, when he came out, saw much people, and was moved with compassion toward them...He answered and said unto them, Give ye them to eat" (Mark 6:34,37).

I read this early in the morning and talked about it at breakfast, saying I thought it was one of the most wonderful miracles in the Bible. Then I began to think of the 2,100 meals a day which we must have to feed our 700 children. I said, "Well, the Lord really provides a miracle every day, right here at the orphanage. Here we sit eating breakfast. We haven't 5 cents and I do not know where it can come from. Yet, I am sure that enough money will come in so that the children will not miss a meal and that will be a miracle because God will be the One to send it." One hour later the mail came and there was an envelope with no letter, only a money order for $50. In the afternoon mail from America, we received $55. When I went to the bank to cash the money, a friend walked in and handed me $5. A stranger stopped me on the street and handed me 50¢. Yesterday $35 came in the mail. A friend walked several miles to bring me $5 last night after dark. This morning another friend telephoned, asking me to send and get beef for the children's supper (worth about $25).

I was telling one of my friends about the beef this evening and he said, "Oh, that reminds me, I have two beefs to send you." His wife handed me $5.

Since we asked for prayer about the salaries for the workers they have been met every month before the time that they had to be paid. But last month came and on the last day of the month there was not enough money to pay all of the salaries; we still owed about $60 or $70.

We said, "Well, this is the first time that we have not been able to pay before the first of the month." The next day, the morning mail brought us a check from an American for $200. We were able to pay up everything, buy all of the needs, and purchase many little things which we had not been able to buy before.

February 8, 1937

We have just had a very lovely visit from some of our friends from the General Council of the Assemblies of God of Springfield, Missouri. Brother J. W. Welch, Brother and Sister E. S. Williams, Brother Noel Perkin, Miss Hattie Hammond and Brother Phil Crouch. For us it was a time never to be forgotten.

When they had all left, I sadly went to my room feeling that a very lovely week had passed forever and most likely I will never see any of them again. I felt so sad and lonesome; I cannot describe it to you. We see lots of Americans here, but not from our church. My work is so far away from all of my friends who help me and they all help me blindly without ever seeing the work, and really know nothing about the work except what I write and tell them.

My family is too big now to be left alone while I go to America, so I am not planning on going back again unless the war or something like that forces me out.

February 15, 1937

Some of you friends will remember that in one of my letters several years ago I wrote and mentioned Lord Maclay of Glasgow, Scotland. He has been a tremendous help to the orphanage over the years in the area of finances. He is now 80 years old, and I received a radiogram from him saying that on February 12 he would arrive in Assiout. We were all too excited for words!

He and his daughter arrived safely and I showed them the orphanage. They were perfectly delighted with everything. That evening before they retired he called me aside and wrote me two checks for $2,500, one for me personally and the other for the orphanage. I could not get to sleep until nearly morning! The next morning after breakfast he called me to him, and asked me a few questions about the possibility of my going to America for a holiday. I told him I was too tired for such a long trip and I get very seasick on the ocean. I told him I would go to a place near here where I could really rest. He said, "Well, Miss Trasher, the Lord spoke to me this morning in my bed and showed me that I had not given you enough. Therefore I am going to give you a check for $20,000 more" — making his donation in all $25,000. Rejoice with me that God has supplied our needs. The expenses of all last year were $18,346.45. We had a balance on hand the first of this year of $31.57.

Lord Maclay and his daughter went with us to the market and bought candy for all of the children and some lovely cloth to make dresses for the little girls. They only stayed one night. Of course, you can picture the children at the orphanage — everybody happy and thankful to God for more than we could ever have dreamed.

I am planning to go to Cairo some day this week and stay in a nice quiet hotel and rest! Lord Maclay was very anxious for me to take care of my health, so for the first time in 27 years I will be able to do so.

March 30, 1937

I am sure you will be glad to hear that the Lord enabled me to get away from Assiout for a whole month's rest. I went to Cairo to a hotel and stayed there 2 weeks. Then a friend of mine who lives in Alexandria invited me to visit her, so I went there for 2 more weeks. I was very thankful to get back to Assiout.

When I returned I found the new storeroom and the new sewing room all finished, and the large new room upstairs over the nursery nearly finished!

My sister, Mrs. Benton, is expecting to come out and visit me this December. I will be so delighted to see her; I have not been home since 1929, but if my sister comes out to see me it will be the next best thing to home. This will be her fourth visit to me (including our first trip together to Egypt in 1910).

She will certainly see some great changes since she was last here. The children are all delighted that their "Aunt Jennie" is coming. She is always a wonderful help to me; I wish it were possible for her to stay. But she cannot do this, so I am thankful that the Lord enables her to give me a year's help every now and then. She knows Arabic and the children love her and mind her. Pray that God may bring her safely to us.

We have just bought several new cows. We have never been able to get enough milk for our large family, but now God has met the need and sent in enough money for us to give the boys and girls the milk they need. We give the extra milk one day to the boys and the next to the girls. A good cow costs about $70 to $75. Food for the cows is very expensive since there are no grassy fields to turn them loose in. We have to keep them tied up in stalls nearly the whole year. We have about seven acres of land, but the buildings take up a large part and then we need the rest for raising vegetables and providing grounds for the children.

Land used to be very cheap here — $500 an acre; now it is about $1,800 and even at that price no one really wants to sell.

When I first built out here, there were no buildings at all, only large fields of corn; no one would dare to build so far away from town! Everyone said that I would be killed the first night if I built so far from town. Now quite a little town has built around us, and the value of land has jumped up from that of farmland to building lots.

June 3, 1937

We have been trying to purchase a strip of land, about one acre, which runs between the main building on our property and the church, nursery, and my cottage. This is owned by nine Egyptian farmers, and we have been trying to get them to sell the whole piece so that all our land will be inside of our high wall. Some are willing to sell, others are holding out for higher prices; they know we are very anxious to buy the land. Pray that the Lord's will be done.

You will be interested to hear that I have opened a nice grocery store for five of the older boys to work in. They are kept busy all day long, and will make quite a nice living in this way.

The store is located on the main street between the post office and the three banks, approximately a block and a half from the railroad station. We only pay $12.50 a month rent. We named it "The Family Grocery."

The missionaries and Christian people like to trade with the boys because there are no wines or whiskey being sold as is done in all of the other grocery stores. We went down and had prayer there the day before the opening that the Lord's blessing might be on all that is done here.

September 14, 1937

The long, hot summer is over and school has started again. Now that the missionaries have returned from their holidays, a friend has invited me to go for 2 or 3 weeks' rest at her home at the seashore; I am planning to go. I feel that this kind offer is surely of the Lord.

I have had the most wonderful summer with the children — the best that I have had in 10 or 15 years. I was able to spend a great deal of time with the girls. We had meetings, sewing circles, long talks, and for the first time in years I had time enough to get in real personal touch with the children. The effect on them has been greater than I ever dreamed it would be.

I made a special garden next to my house and arranged a nice big bedroom. I chose 25 of the most delicate little girls and let them stay 2 weeks, then sent them back and brought another 25.

While they are here I cook the very best food so they will have extra nourishment for their bodies.

I also made a swimming pool for all of the children. We have a large water engine for irrigating our land. And now as the water rushes out of the large pipe, it goes into the pool and then goes to water the land. Many of the children have learned how to swim, and it has meant so much to have a place where they can have a good cool bath during these awfully hot days.

September 27, 1937, is my 50th birthday, and as I see the years passing I know that each passing day brings me nearer to the time when my work among the children will be over. I always pray the Lord will help me in this life. He has given me good health and I thank Him for it.

I am able to see a great change for the better in the children. The older boys and girls now are much more help to me than ever before and I am able to lean on them and leave things entirely in their hands. I am sometimes surprised to see that they have done the job better than I could have done it.

November 11, 1937

I wish I had some exciting reports to write to you about, but our work goes on slowly. It takes a long time for our babies to grow up and many of them, when they do grow up, are just ordinary boys and girls. Sometimes I long to see sweeping results in their lives, but Jesus did most of His work among the simple fisher folks, so we are trying every day to sow the seed in the hearts of these simple little children. We know that He loves them just as much as He loves the great and mighty people of this world.

Instead of getting tired of my work, I love it more than ever and the children are dearer to me. I will never be able to do any great thing in life so I am trying to do as many little things as well as I possibly can. Perhaps when they are all put together they will amount to something. And perhaps the Lord may use some of the boys and girls to do work that I never could have done.

When I was a little girl their age, I am sure that no one ever thought that I would someday be a missionary! I was raised a Catholic and never saw a Bible until I was 16 years old.

One day in Atlanta, Georgia, I went to visit a friend and I saw a book on her table entitled "Holy Bible." I said, "Oh, this is a Bible; I have heard of the Bible." I went home and told my mother that I had seen a Bible, and that I would like very much to have one to read. She promised me one for my birthday which was some weeks off. I asked her if I could have it then, saying that I would not expect anything else for my birthday. She bought it for me.

Oh, the wonder of reading for the first time the precious Word of God! I read it as a beautiful and strange story, never once thinking that it had a personal message for me.

A few months later, on Christmas Day, we had some friends come to spend the evening. Our neighbor knew that we were Catholics but he let his light shine. He quietly began to tell the story of his life, how he once had been very wicked but that God had saved him and changed his whole life.

This was indeed strange news to me. I got a little stool and drew up by his side and never lost a word he said. Then he told us, "We have a little prayer meeting at our house every Wednesday." I asked Mother if I could go. She agreed.

The next day I went to see this man's wife and asked her to tell me some more of this news. She said it was wash day and she was busy. I said, "If you will tell me, I will help with the wash."

A few weeks after that I got down by an old log in the bushes, alone, and prayed until God wonderfully saved my soul. Later my dear mother was saved and she died a true Christian.

One day, several months after I was saved, I went out and picked some wild flowers, found a quiet place, and got down on my knees in the woods and prayed, "Lord, I do wish I had something to give You; I have nothing but these flowers." I gave them to God as solemnly and earnestly as I later gave my life to pick the little Egyptian flowers for His kingdom. I am quite sure He accepted them. So I do not feel discouraged because my work is among simple little girls and boys, for perhaps He really loves most the children who are simple and earnest.

January 1938

Here is an account of some of the food consumed and other items used during the year of 1937 by the 700 children of the orphanage.

Wheat............................... 3,465 bushels
Beans ....315 bushels
Lentils ....315 bushels
Onions ....360 bushels
Garlic..................................2,000 pounds
Soap ....14,000 pounds
Sugar ....8,333 pounds
Syrup ....6,000 pounds
Cooking butter ....2,139 pounds
Oil ....1,944 gallons
Kerosene ....4,000 gallons

One meal of cabbage and tomatoes takes 150 pounds of tomatoes and 100 cabbages.

One acre of Indian corn will make eight meals for the children.

We spent $3,158.52 for cloth during the year.

It would cost me $280 if I gave each child a 10¢ comb, a 5¢ cake of soap, and a 25¢ towel.

January 30, 1938

I am very sorry to have to ask all of my friends who send me packages not to do so. The Egyptian government has made a new rule which says that no missionary or charitable work will again be allowed exemption from duty. If they only charged a small amount it would not matter, but their rates amount to nearly the entire value of the goods in the package. Two small packages of toys recently cost me over $4. I am so sorry about this; we have received such beautiful clothes, and they were such a great help to us. Those who wish to help clothe the children can instead send money.

March 12, 1938

Miss Clayton, an English lady, has been with us at the orphanage since 1928. She gives all of her time to teaching the little girls. Oh, she has been such a wonderful help.

Every day before school she sees all of the sick girls and attends to them before beginning her long day of work in school. Many times she has gone on with her teaching when she should have been in bed. She is the only one who has stood by us year in and year out. Many have come and gone, but this faithful missionary has held on both during the lean years and the fat. And she will share with us when the time of reaping comes. Pray for her that God will give her renewed strength in her body.

Last Sunday afternoon there was a great outpouring of the Spirit of God at our church and the children prayed for nearly 3 hours. Dark came but the lights were not turned on at once. I was kneeling on the platform and when I looked up I could see hundreds of little forms with raised hands, calling out to God in one volume of prayer. No one was thinking of anyone else; it was too dark to see who was near you. But, I don't think I ever had seen before what my call really meant. All the wonder of it was shown to me in a new way; all of the sacrifices of the past years and the hardship seemed to melt into nothing as the glory of the call of God was shown me. He has allowed me to be the one to open this home of light and comfort for such a great mass of praying children. Nothing life could have given me could have compared to this!

Part Three:

The 1940s

1940

People tell me every day, "Oh, you must not take in any more children; you really must not." But what can I do? They come, each with their very sad story, and how can I turn them away? Unless our Heavenly Father has changed, He has promised to supply all of our needs according to His riches in Glory. Will He stop supplying these needs because I take in a new baby who has just lost its mother? Or because I accept a widow who has just been left with four little children? Somehow I feel that He would do just as I have done — crowd them in and welcome them whether we have room or not.

Yesterday morning a man brought me a tiny little girl 40 days old who had just lost her mother. How could I turn her away? We put another bed in the overcrowded nursery, and she is sleeping peacefully in the place where I believe God would have her to be.

Just after the new baby came, one of my little girls came in and said, "Mamma, outside there is a widow with a lot of children. She says she wants you to let her stay with her children."

I went out to see her and I found a half-blind woman with three little boys who looked to be 5, 6, and 7 years old and a sweet little girl about 3 years old. I asked what she wanted. She said, "Their father is dead and the village people told me to take them to the Lord's house, so I have brought them. Please, may I stay with them?"

I asked her why she did not leave the children with me and go back to her village.

She said, "Go back to what? I have nothing there."

I took her in, although we have no room for her. The widow's house, where I made a room for each widow and her young children, now has two widows and their children packed in where there should only be one. But what can I do?

Last year our family increased at the rate of a new child every 3 days. Everybody knows that this is MUCH too much, but it is so hard to turn them away when I am turning them away from the only door of hope that is open for them.

I look at their poor little bodies in rags, uncombed hair, empty stomachs, and see that they are friendless and ignorant. Then I remember that if I say "yes," in a few years these little girls will be reading, writing, serving, praying, and preparing to be the mothers of happy Christian homes.

If I say "no," they go back to villages where no one really wants them or cares if they are fed or not. They will of course grow up with no education at all but what can be picked up by an unwanted orphan on a village street.

Can you see why it is so very hard for me to refuse? The problem is so much bigger than it looks on the surface. We are crowded, and of course we never have any extra money, but does that really matter? I wonder. I may be wrong, but I think that God understands and He will help.

October 17, 1940

The American mail has been held up for several months and only now are a few, long-delayed letters drifting in. Yet during all of these weeks God has met our needs. How thankful we were to God when all of your offerings came through.

Mrs. C. W. Doney, who has been a missionary here in Egypt since 1913, died September 17, 1940. It was indeed a very sad sight to see all of the little girls whom she had been teaching for years with tears streaming down their sad faces. They have indeed lost a friend and a mother. Sister Doney did a long list of good things for the children of her mission, working until she was unable to do another thing. Her whole body just seemed to give out, too tired and worn out to ever build up again. Then she slipped home to her reward, delivered from all of the suffering.

Our school is now running again even though we are having a very hard time getting textbooks and copybooks. There is a paper shortage in Egypt and the prices of books are more than three times the old prices. This war is teaching many of us how to get along with much less of everything, and how to be more careful with all our things. Above all we are learning to be most thankful for our *many* blessings.

July 15, 1942

Through all of the world's suffering and trouble, God has not forgotten the little orphans. And you good friends are standing by me, too. Every time Egypt is mentioned in the dispatches on the radio, I know that you friends are asking God to remember the Egyptian orphans.

Though everything is quiet in the orphanage, we need your prayers. I have always loved 2 Kings 19:14, which says: "And Hezekiah went up into the house of the Lord, and spread it before the Lord." Perhaps the Lord will lay the burden of Egypt on your hearts and you may feel led to put my letter before Him. He understands all of our needs even better than we do, so He will answer as He sees best. God took care of us during the last war and we often have claimed Psalm 91 which reads, "Is anything too hard for the Lord?" And of course not one word of that Psalm failed us.

Though the mails are irregular and slow, the cable with the

donor support funds from the General Council of the Assemblies of God comes right through the first of every month. And the rate of exchange is still very much in our favor. It is only by your help that our doors are always open to new children who need a home and need to be taught the true foundation for life here and in the next world. You will surely share with me in the heavenly rewards for all of the little lives and souls we have been able to bring to Christ. "As his part is that goeth down to the battle, so shall his part be that tarrieth by the stuff: they shall part alike" (1 Samuel 30:24).

My part is really the easiest, because I get such a wonderful reward right here, seeing the children grow up and seeing the results of my work day by day and year by year. You are giving to children whom you will never see, and who will never be able to personally thank you. "Inasmuch as ye have done it unto one of the least of these my brethren, ye have done it unto me" (Matthew 25:40).

September 11, 1942

It is the most wonderful feeling to know that I am needed, and that there are children who feel they could not get along without me.

Last month I had to go to Cairo, the capital city of Egypt, to speak to the YMCA. I spent only one night there (in the home of one of my married girls). Somehow the word got around that "Mamma" was at Faheem's. That evening the house was filled with boys and girls who had lived at the orphanage, along with their children.

As I looked them over, my heart filled with joy. There was William, the son of a blind man, now founder of a very fine school in Sudan...Philip, a professor in a government high school in Alexandria...Zacher, who has just received his B.A. from the Faculty of Arts in Cairo (fourth in his class) ...Edward, now working in the making of airplanes... Robert, William's brother, a finished cabinet maker... Eskander, the representative of a large drug company...

Askery, a clerk in a lawyer's office in Cairo. . .Shokery, a clerk in the English Army, stationed somewhere near Cairo . . .Wadeah, a telephone exchange clerk in the main office in Cairo. . .Gergus, a beginner in the Egyptian State Railway. These with many others were just a few of those now working in Cairo or on holiday there who happened to hear that I was in town. We had such a wonderful time talking of old days. How we all wished it had been daytime so we could have taken a photograph. Such changes!

As I looked at these fine young men, good fathers with solid Christian homes, and their wives, many of them our girls, and all of the little "grandchildren," I felt well repaid for all the work I had done. Remember, you are helping me to do all of this. God bless you.

November 26, 1942

I think you will be interested in hearing something about our tiny infant orphans. They are all well now and getting nice and fat, thanks to special care given them by a very kind Egyptian doctor, Dr. Anwer Hanna. He and his wife often used to drive up to the orphanage with presents for the children, especially for the smaller ones. At that time they had a little daughter the same age as some of my babies whom I always care for in my own room. We enjoyed comparing the babies to see whose had grown the most. Because of these visits, Dr. Hanna's wife also became a very dear friend to us all. A short time later a little son was born to them and Mrs. Hanna died a few days later. Oh, what a shock to us all!

Poor Dr. Anwer stopped coming to see us. Then about a year after his wife's death, our old friend drove up and gave us the good news that his little motherless babies were doing well.

Dr. Hanna went in and saw the rows of beds filled with little babies and God touched his heart. He saw one baby boy who had a fever and asked me what I was doing for him. I said, "Nothing, I had not noticed he was hot."

He said, "Of course not. How can you possibly watch everything? But this is very bad. You must have one of the girls take the babies' temperatures twice a day and have charts for them so you can see in a minute who is ill."

I said, "Yes, Doctor, but when I find they have a fever you will be too far away to see the charts. Shall I mail them to you?" (He does not live in Assiout.)

He replied, "No, I am going to teach you what to do."

He returned to his village and wrote me about 75 pages of instructions, telling me what to do in every possible case of illness. He told me what kind of food to give and how much for all different ages, and sent me special measures for milk, sugar, etc. He wrote these instructions both in Arabic and in English.

Well, we had the charts printed and taught the girls how to take temperatures and fill in the charts. Then the big girls and I started studying the instructions every Monday and Friday afternoon. We have finished now, and we all know what to do for a child when he is ill and in many cases we know what the illness is.

Sometimes when I come home from town, a girl will tell me that a baby is ill. I begin to tell her what to do. She says, "Yes, Mamma, that is exactly what I have done." We have not lost any babies since Dr. Hanna gave us these instructions; all our babies are fat and healthy now.

February 11, 1943

Many times as our pastor preaches, I sit on the platform and try to imagine each little girl and boy as they will be in a few years, teaching their children what they are learning today.

One day I was in Cairo and I thought I would visit one of my married girls. As I was passing under the window, I heard the mother calling to her child, "Honey, come here." Honey! Where had that word come from? That word belongs only in Georgia or Florida, but here it was in Cairo!

Then I smiled as a warm feeling went all over me. I had brought that little part of the dear old south over here, plus a whole lot more that will be a part of Egypt someday when I and all who ever knew me are gone. We are planting seeds in the very best ground, in the hearts of little children, and they cannot do anything but pass it on! For what does a child pass on but the things he has learned? And here we are day after day and year after year teaching them the things of God, and life, and decency. "Train up a child in the way he should go, and when he is old he will not depart from it" (Proverbs 22:6).

All of this, you are helping me to do. Your name may not be mentioned and your gift may be forgotten, but our loving Father does not forget even a cup of cold water given in His name.

April 13, 1943

We live a long way from town and have to use our car many times a day. Recently our tires began to wear out. We were unable to buy any more, so we applied to the government in Cairo, but they did not have any our size. We wrote to some of our friends, but no one could help us. So we patched our old ones as best we could. But nearly every time we went to town the tires went flat. Two of them were very good, nearly new, but the others were no good at all and were patched so that the bumping was awful. The black market had offered us a pair for $250, but we refused.

A young South African soldier who knew about our failure to obtain tires said, "Well, now what are you going to do?"

I said, "Well, we will pray." The next day I went back to Assiout. There was my car waiting at the station with two brand new tires! Why, I hadn't even had time to pray about it!

My heart is filled with joy this morning as I look over the place and see how wonderfully the Lord is blessing us in every department of the work. But it is not only I who can see what the Lord is doing.

Last Saturday a young New Zealand soldier came and asked to look over the orphanage. He saw everything. Then I realized he was very hungry for the Word of God and I asked him to stay for supper that we might have more time to talk; he had to go back to Cairo the next day.

As he left me that evening, he said, "Well, now I can go back and stand the horrors of war; my whole life has been changed by what I have seen here. I know God sent me to meet you and see what you are doing."

Many of the dear soldiers say the same thing, that their sight of the mission work being done in Assiout has changed their whole lives. May God bless you for helping me to continue it all.

1945

All of my mail has been badly neglected since I broke my left elbow. One night about a month ago I was in bed asleep when the telephone rang. It was one of my boys saying he had just arrived in Assiout and would like to come spend the night. I got up and prepared him some supper, then went out to the storeroom to get some other things. There was a large bench in the yard which I did not see; I hit it very hard and fell on my elbow and broke it. I was operated on and two of the broken bones were taken out. I am all right now, but my arm is very stiff and painful. Pray that God will give me the use of my arm again for I have much work to do.

We never have had running water in any of the buildings but we are planning now to have it installed. There is no water system on our side of the river so we will have to make our own. This will be expensive at first but well worth it in the long run. We already have the engine; we still need the pipes and tanks.

Our new hospital is nearly finished and we already have started using part of it. We hope to have it all finished next month. It certainly will be a blessing to me to be able to remove the sick children from my house. It is so wonderful to be able to get back to my work again, even if I can use only one hand! There is nothing like good health and plenty of good work to do!

Left: Miss Lillian as a young woman. She was born Lillian Hunt Trasher on September 27, 1887, in Jacksonville, Florida, and was appointed as an Assemblies of God missionary on November 18, 1919. She died on December 17, 1961, in Assiout, Egypt.

Right: Lillian Trasher (left) and her sister Jennie in 1910, leaving America for the first time. Below: Lillian Trasher (left) and Jennie Benton on February 10, 1961 — the 50th anniversary of the orphanage.

*Right: Mamma Lillian,
1954, in her office where
she handled orphanage
business.*

*Below: Mamma Lillian
returning to Egypt in
1955 after a brief
furlough.*

Left: These babies were special to Mamma Lillian because they had been completely abandoned.

Above: The children playing in front of the new hospital (1952).

Above: Clark Memorial Church, 1953, at the orphanage. Below: The children welcome back Mamma Lillian and Aunt Jennie in 1955.

Left: Everyone enjoyed unpacking barrels from the Women's Missionary Council.

Above: A view of the orphanage buildings from the water tower. Below: The widows prepared about 3,600 meals a day in this kitchen (photo about 1960).

Above: The children enjoy a swim on a hot day with Mamma (1954). Below: The babies were Mamma Lillian's special concern.

Right: Many children were taught by Mamma Lillian over the years. Below: Orphanage boys dressed as prophets read from the Scriptures in an Easter drama (1956).

Right: These were the boys at the orphanage in 1944 (not counting babies). Below: This widow with five children found a home at the orphanage.

Left: Fouzeah Gindy and her sister Ida upon arrival at the orphanage in May 1943. Below: The same girls in 1954.

Above: George Assad (at pulpit) in 1959 at his ordination; Lillian Trasher and T. F. Zimmerman are seated behind him.

Right: A 1961 photo of Miss Lillian with T. F. Zimmerman, general superintendent (left), and J. Philip Hogan, executive director of the Division of Foreign Missions.
Below: Former Prime Minister of Egypt, Mohammed Naguib, giving cakes to babies in March 1953.

Above: George Assad, director of the orphanage, with his wife and three of his children.

Below: Female residents of the orphanage enjoy a time of outdoor fellowship.

Above: Contented babies at play in the new nursery.

Below: Orphanage girls have plenty of "sisters."

Dwight Dobson Photo

Above: Haircutting time at the orphanage. Left: A blind lady reading Scripture.

George Assad Photo

Above: A game of basketball is fun for players and spectators.

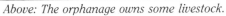

Above: The orphanage owns some livestock.

Widows are pictured preparing large quantities of bread dough and eggplant.

David Irwin **Photos**

Below: A portion of the orphanage grounds.

Above: One of the orphanage choirs being directed by Reverend Joseph Habib, who grew up in the home and was graduated from Bible school.

Above: The orphanage director, George Assad (in brown suit) is accompanied by (left to right) Missionary Robert Creel; the governor of Assiout; and orphanage board chairman Ramses El Masry on February 11, 1983, the 72nd anniversary of the opening of the home. Missionary Gordan Barnett is pictured behind Brother Creel and to his left. On this occasion, Brother Creel, Assemblies of God area representative for the Middle East and North Africa, received an award of honor given to the Lillian Trasher Memorial Orphanage by Egypt's Ministry of Social Affairs. Twelve thousand friends of the orphanage were on hand to share in the festivities.

April 13, 1945

I am very sad to tell you that the Lord saw fit to call home my dear co-worker, Miss Harriett Clayton. She has worked with me for about 17 years. She was indeed a mother to the children. Thank God the older boys and girls are now quite able to take on the work where she left off.

The teaching and work will continue, but no one will be able to fill her place in the hearts of the girls.

Two little boys have been brought to the orphanage just since I started writing this letter. I am quite sure that I have never seen children dressed in such rags. One is about seven and the other about eight, sweet little faces looking in wonder at everything. Oh, the joy of being able to take such little boys and give them a bath, plus the first real clothes they have ever had.

I never get over the thrill of a "new child." They come from having nothing to having everything they need. It is just the other way around in America. A child loses his parents and his home of love and care, and is put into an institution where he loses all the home life he has been used to. It is a real blow that he may never get over.

Our dear little children are for the first time entering real home life when they come to the orphanage. The change comes quickly — with plenty of good food, clean clothes, kind friends — and soon the soul inside the body learns of God and His love.

1945

I have been trying for several years to buy a strip of land next to our church, but the owners have absolutely refused to sell. This week one man decided to let me have a little strip. After he sold this piece to me, others decided that they had better sell too, in case the price goes down now that the European war is over. So, thank God, after all these years we have at least been able to buy nearly an acre.

We need land so much for our buildings, playgrounds, garden, and vegetables, as well as land for cows. With this new land, we now have about eight acres. Because of our many large buildings we do not have space left for a garden and fruit growing, which we need so much. Land is very hard to buy at any time in Egypt; it is scarce and very expensive. No one likes to sell land for it will be difficult for them to ever replace it.

We have had to make a lot of changes since the death of Miss Clayton; she was in charge of the girls. The girls' building is about two blocks away from me. This was all right as long as Miss Clayton was watching over them, but we have decided to move the widows over to the girls' building and put the girls in their building. There are so many girls that we have had to make the widows' building nearly twice as large as it was. Nearly everything is finished now but the painting and two or three doors and windows. The Lord has met all of the needs for the enlargement and improvements. The place is really beautiful and the widows will have a much larger building with a large garden. The girls will now be directly under my care.

December 11, 1945

We are very delighted to be able to buy a lot of supplies from the American Army these days. They are giving the American missionaries first chance to purchase such items as food, dishes, mattress covers, thread, beds, and blankets.

We are not allowed to buy anything with Egyptian money, and of course we cannot get American money here. So I have arranged with Brother Noel Perkin from the Foreign Missions Department in Springfield, Missouri, to pay the War Department in Washington with the money that comes in designated for the orphanage. This is a wonderful chance because items from the army are much better and much cheaper than they are in the local Egyptian market.

Measles have started again at the orphanage! This is the hardest illness we have had to contend with. It lingers long, spreads quickly, and leaves some of the babies so weak.

The new hospital is wonderful, large and comfortable, bright and cheerful, and just near enough to my cottage to make it easy for me to run in and out without any effort at all.

Having the girls moved over to the widows' building has made it easy for me to be in contact with all of the girls now. At first only the babies were with me, but now I conduct the morning chapel service for the girls. I feel that it is my greatest chance to plant the Word of God in their hearts.

D.D.T. has come to Egypt! We are not allowed to buy it yet, but yesterday the government sent several men and women to do some of the rooms. Oh, it is wonderful. . .not a fly this morning! We are all just waiting for the time when we will be allowed to buy all we need. It will surely be one of the greatest blessings to have something to fight these awful pests.

January 20, 1946

Today I have been thinking of Luke 9:47 where it says: "And Jesus, perceiving the thought of their heart, took a child, and set him by him."

A child. . .the most valuable thing in the world. It is the child who will carry on when we are gone. The boys and girls will run the world and be the ones to spread the gospel when we have finished our work. What a responsibility it is for us whom God has given the privilege of teaching and molding the lives and souls of little children. What a thrill to think of the dormant possibilities waiting to wake up in the lives of the hundreds of boys and girls whom God has given to me. Oh, the wonder of the minute when the soul of a child wakes up and for the first time feels the urge to do something great or to be someone greater than he is. Most of them cannot express it, and we who long to see them grow in spiritual things grow weary and discouraged and often wonder why we see so little results. But we are wrong; the seed is there and will have its effect on the child's life even though we may not see it at once. As the years pass we can look back and see what God has done.

Pray for me as I try to plant the living Word in their hearts.

There are so many other things which must be done in a home full of hundreds of children — sewing, school-teaching, caring of the babies, meeting visitors, keeping the home and the children clean, buying the food and clothes, seeing about the money, and — the hardest of all for me — keeping my mail answered.

This is the first time in years that the measles started and did not spread; we had only a few light cases. This is because with our new hospital we were able to isolate children with measles instead of keeping them in my house as I was obliged to do in all of the past years.

March 27, 1946

We are again having to make quite a few changes in our buildings. The orphanage faces a canal with a small private road between our buildings and the canal. The government has decided to widen the canal, which will mean taking the road and the whole face of two of our buildings. One building is not too important so we will just tear it down, but the other is the main building where the boys live. We will have to move back our fence to make a new road and we already have started to build another large building for the boys.

Just before we started building, one of my Egyptian friends gave me $500 in memory of her brother who had just died. Another friend gave me $1,000 also in memory of the same young man who was very much loved by everybody in Assiout.

I wish you could have been with us last week at our communion service. The Spirit of the Lord was surely there in a wonderful way. Children were weeping and praying all over the church.

Brother Brown, who has just returned to the Lord's work here in Egypt after being in America during the war, told me after the service that he had never seen such a sight in all his life. I said to his wife, "Well, Sister Brown, we are planting the seed. Someday we will see the results."

She said, "These are the results!" As I thought over what she had said, it dawned on me that she was right. What more do we want than to see souls crying out to God? We plant the seed but it is He who will give the increase. We cannot follow these children all through their lives, but we can give them the right start and then when they no longer have us to depend upon, they will be able to call upon God directly for help.

April 24, 1946

When we hear of the great suffering of the poor in other countries, we bow our heads in thanks to God for His great kindness to us and our hundreds of orphan children; they have never missed a meal. May God bless you for standing by me and the children.

We had such a lovely Easter this year, the most wonderful one we have ever had. We woke the children up at 4 a.m., washed and dressed them in their very best clothes, and then went out in one of our fields for our first Easter sunrise service.

One of the teachers read the Easter story in the Bible. Then I told the children the account of the death and resurrection of Christ. The older boys prayed and then the children sang lovely songs until the sun was up.

Everyone came over to my cottage then for breakfast. We had 2,300 eggs. Each child got two eggs, bread and onions, and a cup of warm milk. Oh, it was a wonderful day!

Dinner, too, was a wonderful meal. I had bought two large calves and someone sent a sheep. One family sent a quarter of beef, another sent half a cow, another a goat leg, someone else another quarter of beef. There was nothing left over.

I nearly forgot to tell you that another friend sent us a very large ox for which he paid $180. As it had not been butchered, we kept it for another day. The children all said they had never had such an Easter before. The Egyptian Easter is the greatest feast of the year, even larger than Christmas.

After dinner one of our boys announced his engagement to one of the girls. The Egyptians call an engagement "half marriage." After the engagement service we had a wedding; one of our girls married one of our boys. The young man is a Pentecostal preacher. That night we had another wedding — the daughter of our pastor was married. By the time I got home and went to bed I was a bit tired! Tired, but very happy.

May 20, 1946

Last week we had such a wonderful time; a total of 267 young people from the orphanage were baptized. It was a beautiful sight to see all the older girls dressed in new white dresses marching from the church to the swimming pool, then the smaller girls. After the girls had been baptized, the boys marched up. Brother and Sister Gutel from Cairo and Brother and Sister Brown from Assiout came to help me with the baptizing.

We had some lovely meetings prior to the baptismal service, all of the young people calling out to God to clean their hearts in readiness for baptism. Several of the blind girls testified of how God had convicted them and saved them.

Sometimes it is a long road to travel from the time we take in a new baby to the day we see spiritual results. But when I saw all of those young girls and boys marching out to publicly take a stand for God, I forgot all of the years between and thanked God that I had been able to help them. The time and the wait were surely worth it in the end.

July 25, 1946

I am sure you will be very pleased to hear that God is giving us a real revival here at the orphanage among all ages.

Last night we had a very blessed meeting. Boys and girls all over the church were standing to tell how they had been great "sinners" but now had given their hearts to God.

One little girl about 11 years old, whom I raised from a newborn baby, has a Bible study out in the garden every night after supper. A few days ago the girls came to me saying that it was too dark to read the Bible. That was soon settled by getting one of the blind girls to read for them!

All of the blind girls can read the Bible in Braille. They take turns reading at evening prayers at the girls' building. And they read to the sick in the hospital. Miss Annie Lamberton, who was a missionary here with me some years ago, taught herself Braille so she could teach the blind girls. She had to be sent back to America because of illness, but her great work still goes on. The girls now read all of the books of the Bible as well as the children who can see.

September 9, 1946

Our revival at the orphanage is still going on. It started in May and has continued all through the summer. There is such a difference in the older girls. They are all wanting to do something to help "pass it on." Some are holding meetings with the widows, others read and pray with the sick in the hospital, another is in charge of those who wish to tarry for the baptism of the Holy Ghost.

The older boys are holding special meetings for the boys who are seeking God. When there is a call for prayer, it is indeed like the "sound of many waters." There is one thing for sure: every child raised in the orphanage knows how to call upon God.

Everything is in a great rush to get ready for the opening of school. The summer has been long and hot and I am indeed glad that it is over. The heat is very hard on me now; I am not as young as I once was! I will be 59 years old this month. Thank God my health is much better this year than it was last year. And the older girls and boys are able to help me a lot now. I feel that it will be such good training for them in their own lives. I really believe that they enjoy helping me as best they can.

December 17, 1946

As you will remember the government is going to widen the canal in front of our orphanage, and our old building will have to be torn down. We decided we would have to build another building before the old one was taken down.

Our new main building is now finished except for the painting.

We were not using the girls' old building as we had moved the girls over near me after Miss Clayton died, so we tore it all down and used the material for the new building.

But it had to be much larger so it cost us a lot of money to buy the extra materials, but thank God the whole building is now finished and we do not owe anything on it.

Because of the shortage of cloth in Egypt, the Egyptian Charity Society has been giving out a large stock of old clothes from the Egyptian Army. They gave us some last year and they have just given me 1,000 more pieces. We are very thankful to get them as most of the suits are woolen, but oh it is an awful, dirty job turning and cutting all of those old suits. Yet when we see the children nice and warm, we don't mind the extra work.

Last March the Charity Society asked us if we would help make over some of the suits for other poor schools in Assiout. We made 3,400. Words cannot describe what a job it was! Many of our married girls came every day to help us, and we did it in 3 weeks.

February 19, 1947

Thank you so much for your gifts to the orphanage. The gifts which you and other friends in America are able to send make it possible for me to put all of my time and energy on the children instead of worrying about food and expenses.

In past years I had to spend the greater part of my time and strength getting money for their needs. It seems that God sees that I now would not be able to travel in all of the hundreds of little villages riding on a donkey as I used to do. I was young then.

This past year has been different from any of the past years. I have felt the call to "redeem the time" as never before in my life. Our pastor, Reverend Habib, used to take both of the

Sunday services, but I asked him to let me take the afternoon meeting. I have done this now for some time, as well as conducting the Friday night prayer meeting and giving a short talk to the girls at chapel service every morning before school.

Also, every morning I teach two classes of English. Then at 3:30 to 5:30 p.m. I teach French reading and translation. Every evening but Friday (prayer meeting night) and Sunday nights, I have a class for my teacher girls from 7 to 9 p.m.

These two hours are more joy to me than any part of my work. There are 18 girls, and they are educated enough so that it is no strain on me to teach them, and we study books that I myself enjoy. I have these classes in my office. We all feel that we are not really doing school work but just enjoying a lovely evening.

I now feel that I must try to pass on everything I can to the children while I am able to do it. This is the part of me which will live long after me. I am trying so hard to pass on all that I can of the good which God has given me, things which will live in the children and be passed down to their children. I feel that it is a great loss to let anything good die if it can be made to live by passing it on to others.

February 26, 1947

This has indeed been a most exciting week. Miss Florence Christie and Miss Katherine Burt have just arrived from America; they were held up in New York for such a long time. Oh, the excitement of all the family! The older girls all ran up to see if Miss Christie could remember their names. The new ones sidled up to get a look at Miss Christie, of whom they had heard so much.

Miss Burt, who has come for the first time, stood by enjoying the sight until things quieted down enough for her to ask some questions, using the Arabic which she had learned from Miss Christie.

The Sunday service was more than a success; Miss Burt had brought her accordion with her. How the children love music.

Then both women spoke to the children and delivered messages from our many friends in America. After things quieted down a bit, we were able to open the boxes of lovely presents which had been sent from friends at home. A lovely radio for me! We will all enjoy it. Spoons, a coffee pot, a pressure cooker, but the crowning gifts were the wonderful clothes for the children! Beautiful suits for boys, lovely dresses for the little girls, and baby clothes. Oh, they were just too lovely for words!

We are all delighted with the new plans for the children to get more out into the Lord's work. Next week all of the missionaries are going to meet in Cairo to study this great plan. We know of course that our boys will need some practical training, a special Bible course and more education before getting into the work. After having that they will need someone to oversee the village work which they will be doing.

Our highest class at the orphanage is about like the 8th grade in America. The new Bible school will be in Cairo. Then we are hoping that Miss Christie and Miss Burt will oversee the new works with the boys as they leave the Bible school.

We have 12 boys here now ready to go after school closes in May. Four of these boys are in high school in Assiout, having finished our orphanage school. Pray for us that God will guide us in the best way.

Part Four:

Mamma's Last Years

December 21, 1951

As it is quite cold here these days, we have been very busy giving out shoes and warm clothes. We have two shoemakers working all year to try to get enough shoes ready for winter.

The little children are allowed to go barefooted during the hot summer, but of course the older children have to have shoes all year around. Last year we were able to buy a large number of woolen pajamas from the American Army here. We have worked very hard indeed to make coats out of them for the children. We have just finished making one for each child, but that is not enough. All of the smaller children must have two each.

We never, never finish sewing; dozens of girls have to make at least one garment each, every day. The cutting is an awful job! I really think though that washing clothes is the biggest job of the whole orphanage. The washing for the tiny infants alone begins early in the morning and goes on until night. If visitors come in the evening there is a rush to grab up baby clothes from off the tables and chairs all over the house where we are trying to get them dry enough for use!

I now have 29 of these smallest babies (under walking size).

Two of them have just learned to walk. We are all delighted and hope a lot more will soon be joining the "big babies."

This is the largest number of babies we have ever had at one time. I feel that we have been able to save the lives of many of the small delicate infants by having them right here in my house where I can give them personal care. I also have been able to give practical teaching to the girls in charge of the babies.

We have been able to continue the work on the new building and we feel sure that the money will continue to come in sufficiently. More money always comes in around Christmas. Some send early and some send just at Christmas. The Egyptians hold January 7 as Christmas, so we have two Christmases each year! Really, the orphans do have a lovely time receiving oranges, candy, meat, and toys. We also bought a whole truckload of peanuts for them.

Schools from all over the Assiout District come to see the orphanage. Muslim boys' and girls' schools, Catholic and all different kinds of schools send their students to see the orphanage. It takes about an hour to tour the place. The students and the teachers seem to enjoy it very much indeed. Quite a number of the children give donations to the orphanage.

Last week the Government Tourist Agency sent a representative to arrange with me for the orphanage to be put on the official list of places to be shown to tourists. This we trust will be a blessing both to us and the people who come to see us.

March 2, 1952

Giving out candy is a lovely sight! Hundreds of little hands all trying to reach me, all trying to get something very precious. One cannot see the faces, only hundreds of trembling hands — baby hands, little girl and boy hands, and little inky fingers just learning how to hold a pen. Some hands are so small they cannot hold the precious candy and it falls to the ground. Then there is the tragedy of those children who come too late, after all has been given out.

Oh, those little hands! What a lot they expect of us and how many times we will have to fill them. How many times the choice bits will fall to the ground before the children grow up, but someday they will be able to give to others.

We sometimes feel so swamped and overcome with numbers. Everything would be easy if there were not quite so many. In everything the children have to "wait their time."

If a gift of meat comes in, it seldom is enough for everybody. So those who do not get meat today may have to wait several days or longer before their turn comes around. But perhaps this, in itself, will be a good lesson for them later in life.

Once, during the past days when we never knew where the next meal would come from (this condition truly went on for years!), a kind friend said, "Lillian, why do you keep on taking in new children when you have so many needs for the children whom you already have?"

I told her that I saw her point, but at the same time the new children were so badly in need of just anything I could give them that I found it impossible to turn them away. If we waited until extra money came in, we would never do anything. There never was any extra money! I always have kept on taking in new children who needed to be here, and all of those who have come in have been cared for. Each year things have improved: a better school (last year our Girls' School got the highest grades of all Assiout schools and our Boys' next highest), better food, better and warmer clothes, more buildings, and much better health.

We never have waited until we had enough money to begin anything. We only waited until we were sure that we needed it and that the project was God's will. Once that was settled, we could and did expect God's blessing on whatever we undertook. In my 41 years here, there never has been any unfinished undertaking at the orphanage. It has been very wonderful working with God as our Head, Leader, Advisor, and Friend.

April 1952

We are able to look about us and see a happy, joyful home where children play, work, and learn together. Buildings have sprung up until the appearance of the home is like a small village, where needs of more than 800 are met daily in a reoccurring miracle. We rejoice and give thanks for all this to a loving Heavenly Father who has moved on your hearts to give that these little ones might be cared for.

These are busy days here. The school year is nearing the end and the children are working very hard.

The beautiful new hospital building that we have been working on is now finished and is such a blessing. The building that used to be the hospital now serves as a nursery for our babies.

With the completion of this building project we are ready for our next. It seems impossible that the day will ever come when everything is caught up and we can sit down and relax. But with so many children to see about we cannot expect anything else.

With the babies well taken care of now, we are turning our attention to the widows. We had drawn tentative plans for a special building for the widows, but recently a very good idea has come to us. The building where we have our kindergarten already houses some of the widows, and with very little changing this building can be turned into a very comfortable widows' home. We all agree that it could not be more ideal for the widows if we had specially constructed it for this use.

And the kindergarten (which includes the first 3 years of school in Egyptian schools) has always been in a rather unhandy location. It is at the farthest corner of the orphanage, somewhat apart from the other schools, far from the nurseries and far from the teachers' quarters. So here is our plan. We will build a second floor on to our church for classrooms for all of these grades, thus saving valuable land.

Not only will the kindergarten be in a better location, but

our construction costs will be cut in half or more. Furthermore, our church, which has a very thin roof and is unbearably hot in the long summer months, will now be made much cooler with the addition of a floor above it. Also, our church has become too small as our family has increased, and it can now be enlarged so all can be comfortably seated. Plans are being drawn now so that work can be started at once. It is summer now and we can have open-air services for 6 months, and this will be plenty of time for the work to be completed.

The Lord has given us the assurance of His approval on this plan and we know He will see that all will be provided for.

July 1952

Summer has started and school will soon be out. We are all very busy just now with final examinations, and I think we will all be pleased when school is over. The government required the schools to remain open longer this year because the students lost a lot of valuable time during the uprisings, especially those attending the schools in Cairo. Thank God everything is quiet and peaceful now.

We have started work on the enlargement of the church so we are holding our services in the courtyard of the kindergarten until our church is ready for use again. Of course this courtyard is too small to hold all our children so we have divided the family, holding a service first for the older children and then a service for the smaller ones.

I was thrilled this week when I attended the closing exercises of the 185 children in our kindergarten. These tiny tots have been taught by Mrs. Crouch and the older girls working with her. What a marvelous amount of Bible verses they knew. After they started saying their verses they kept going until I thought there would be no end to the number they knew. We feel that when these children become men and women, these words of God will come back to them.

January 11, 1953

As the children run and play in the garden, they look just like any other children. But as I told them last week in church, "You children are different! You are chosen children. Of all of the thousands of orphans in Egypt, God has chosen you to come and be raised in this home which He built for you years before you were born. He prepared a mother to take the place of your mother who in His wisdom was not to live."

I do not know why the Lord sends these children, or what they will do when they grow up, but He has told us to plant the seed and water the young plants and He will give the increase!

As we are shown the childhood pictures of our greatest men in history, none of them *look* great. They stand stiffly in their old-fashioned clothes with simple childish faces and little resemblance to the great persons they later became.

As I sit in church I try to visualize what the different boys and girls will look like 10 or 15 years from now, or what they will be doing then. It is hard for me to see very far ahead when I watch some of the smallest ones sitting on their low baby benches in front of the older children, and watch them squirm and slyly pinch the little ones next to them to pass the time away when the preacher talks too long! But they are getting the Word of God and sometime, somewhere it will spring up and bear fruit, if not in them then in their children.

The Word of God is alive and will not die. We were not asked to give the results; that is for God to do. Man may be able to carve a beautiful statue but it is only God who can breathe into man the breath of life.

The last baby we took in was in a very pitiful condition. She was only 3½ months old. While the papers were being filled out, one of the older girls bathed the baby. She looked so warm, sweet, and clean. I took her in to see her father and the woman who had brought her. When I held the baby out to them, they looked at me and at the baby and had no idea who I was showing them. The woman spoke up and said, "Who is that child?"

I said, "Why, don't you know her? She is the one you just gave us. We have bathed her." They really had no idea who it was!

Many are delicate and ill when they arrive and sometimes we are not able to raise them. But if they do die, I am quite sure that from the day they came to me until God took them home they had the best loving care anyone could have given them. You see my babies are not orphans to me but the dearest things I have in my life; they *are* my life.

March 16, 1953

I am pleased to send you some pictures which I feel sure will interest you. They will give you a better idea than anything I can say of the work you are supporting.

One of these pictures is of William Niseem. Let me tell you William's story. He came here with his little brother and sister. Their father was a blind man and their mother had died of tuberculosis. When their father died too, there was no one to care for them. I took them in and put them in our school. The little girl died later of tuberculosis, but the boys got along fine.

Robert, the younger brother, was not an outstanding scholar, but he finished his grammar school and afterward learned the trade of cabinet making. He did very well indeed and after finishing his training he went to Cairo for employment. During the war Robert worked with the English Army making airplane parts.

William was an exceptional student. We put him through the American college and he became a teacher. Later he went to Sudan and opened a school there. Not long ago we were thrilled to hear over the radio of the important work of this school and the credit it is given in Sudan. In the final government examinations given at the end of the school year, every student passed.

When I saw the picture of our son William and his fine

Sudan students who had made such a good scholastic record, I was thrilled beyond words. I often wonder what would have become of William and Robert and the many other boys and girls like them if they had not found a home in the orphanage.

Long ago, when I first opened the orphanage and for years afterward, I always kept the youngest children in my rooms. Then as I grew older and took a more active part teaching English in the girls' school, I found I had to give over much of the care of the babies to the older girls. But with the arrival of baby Munera, I decided I had better change back again. I knew I was no longer able to carry some of the heavier work, long hours of teaching, and the cutting of clothes for the entire family of 900. So I started working again where my heart has always been — with the babies. Since that day when little Munera was brought to me, I have kept all of the tiny babies with me.

At first they were all in my house. But the number grew so rapidly that later when we made a new hospital we transformed the old building, which was close to my office, into another nursery. Day before yesterday we got our 50th baby!

October 22, 1953

We have had 75 new orphans and widows come in during the last 3 months! Of course many leave us as the new ones come in. The girls marry and the boys go out to work. Often, after the boys find work they come home and ask for one of the girls in marriage. We then have a nice wedding in our big church and they leave to start a new home and family of their own. Other boys, who have widowed mothers, soon take their mothers and younger brothers and sisters and care for them, thus making room for new children who need to come to us.

Three days ago we took in a very poor little boy. His arm and hand are all shriveled up and he does not walk properly. He is not an orphan but his parents are very, very poor and he was dropped from school because the teacher said the other boys laughed at him. Well, we took him and no one here even thinks of laughing at him. The children here all like to help each other.

We have another little boy who came to us when his two legs were cut off by a train. We had artificial legs made for him, but he feels more comfortable without them. All the boys just love to take him to school and church in his little wagon. No one ever thought of laughing at him either.

I have another crippled boy who went through college and has been a preacher of the gospel for several years now.

Lateefa Beshay, a blind girl, is now one of my very best English teachers. She sits in the room and listens to me read and explain the lesson. In a few minutes she understands it perfectly and is able to take the slower children out in another room and teach them so that when they come to me I have been saved most of the hard work.

Henanna Leas, a very sweet little Christian girl, has finished high school after having kept at the head of her class all her high school days. She came to me a poor girl with only stubbs for hands; she had fallen in a fire when a baby. I sent her to the government hospital here in Assiout where the doctors did a very wonderful job on her left hand. She was at last able to hold a spoon or pen, even a needle. She is now a teacher in our school and loved by everybody. It is a wonderful work to be able to take such poor children and give them a chance in life to be as other children and to grow up even to be a very great help to me.

January 16, 1954

The total operation expense of the orphanage for 1953 was $59,436, and we started the new year with a family of 800. This includes 22 blind girls, 80 widows, and 71 babies. Our boys and girls then make up the full 800 God has given us to take care of and train.

Everybody who comes to see the orphanage for the first time says the same thing, "I have heard such a lot about the orphanage, but I never dreamed it was like this. Why, it is a town in itself!"

Yes, it is like a very happy town with our lovely church and three schools — one for the girls, one for the boys, and the kindergarten for the little tots.

You will be pleased to hear that the government has now started to help us by paying the salaries of our schoolteachers. This of course saves us a very large sum of money. The government officials are really very friendly toward us and give no trouble at all; of course, they can see what we are doing for their little orphan children. The president of Egypt visited us last year and said many nice things about our work. This helped to give the people of Egypt a more friendly feeling toward us. About half of our support comes from our kind Egyptian friends.

The Egyptian Christmas is on January 7 so the friends who know that our Christmas is December 25 start then to send presents to the children — peanuts, oranges, candy, clothes, and even cakes. This year a very kind Muslim family came and brought 800 lovely cakes, all covered with icing and fresh from the oven. Another gentleman in Cairo sent a toy for each one. Meat is sent in all day long; some send a sheep, another a nice leg of mutton, another a whole beef. Some young girls in Cairo knitted woolen jackets for about half the babies.

The manager of the National Bank of Assiout and all of his staff came to see the children and brought 100 yards of lovely cloth to make coats for the children and brought the children two oranges each. The Rotary Club also came on Christmas morning bringing cloth, oranges, and a bag of candy for every child.

In the early days, I started around the first of December making pretty dolls so the children would have something "Mamma" had made. Most of the girls helped me do the sewing and stuffing. Those were wonderful days they will never forget.

We still have to ask you not to send packages, as the cost of customs is too high for us to accept the packages. Only books are free of duty.

Our watchnight service was really very lovely. The older children all crowded in our large office, bedrooms, and nurseries which have large double doors that open up. They sat packed all over the floor and sang and sang. About 10 p.m. we started the service with prayer and a "New Year's talk." Then Mr. Crouch showed slides of the life of Christ from the manger to the Cross, followed by a time of communion. At 5 minutes to 12 everyone got down on their knees and waited in perfect silence in prayer until the large office clock solemnly struck the old year out and the new year in. Then I prayed, after which we all got up and wished each other a happy New Year.

On New Year's morning we got a little month-old baby who had just lost her mother. So you see, we have started the new year in the right way!

May 1954

I am enclosing a picture of some of our older girls in our garden at the orphanage. If you look closely, you will notice that each girl is holding one of our small infants. In looking over our records, I find that last month we got 10 new babies; only one of them can walk. This child is 2 years old and her baby sister is 6 months old. They came to the orphanage last week because one of the brick walls of their house fell down. The poor mother, who was standing by the wall, was crushed so badly that the doctors say she will never be able to walk again. How thankful the family is that they don't have to worry about the children as well as the poor suffering mother. I am always so thankful that God has enabled us to make a home for such poor, helpless little ones.

Those children who came in April include a girl 1 day old, a boy 12 days old, and another baby girl 25 days old, and a girl 2 months old. There were two little boys over a year old, and when they came they were nothing but skin and bones. They could hardly hold up their heads. Now both are sitting up and gaining nicely.

Of course, in addition to the babies, a number of widows and older boys and girls came in during the past month!

We are planning to have a baptismal service in our swimming pool next week. The pastor of the town church wants to have some of his members baptized, and before the close of the school year we always like to baptize those who have not yet been baptized, so we are going to have a joint service this year. It is always a very touching scene, seeing the young boys and girls taking a public stand for God. We also have the annual service for the older children who have not yet joined the church. They come forward and are received into the church and their names are put on the list of church members.

This list is on the wall in the back of the church. Before they are allowed to join, Reverend Crouch works with them for many weeks to prepare them for membership and to help them understand more clearly the teachings of our church.

At the end of each school year we lose a lot of our older boys and girls. The girls get married and the boys go out to whatever work they are able to do. It is very important that they give their hearts to God and are baptized before they leave us. We like to give a new Bible to all of the older students so they can keep them when they leave. Pray for us that we may be able to plant the seed in their hearts so they will want to serve God when they have to leave the orphanage and go out to face the evils of a cold world.

June 1956

A number of our older girls and boys have left us lately, but new ones are quickly taking their places. Just since I returned from America, I have taken in 27 babies in my two nurseries. This, of course, does not count all of the older orphans who have come in and two older blind women.

Our buildings are all packed — there is not a corner in which to put another bed. And what are we going to do? Build! We are building a very large dining room and will use the old dining room for a bedroom for our new little girls coming in all the time.

We have just finished a second floor to our hospital. We have made a lovely laundry room with a large heating system for the water. The church in Baytown, Texas, gave us two automatic washing machines so we got busy and installed electricity and hot water in the nursery laundry. I have heard that the washing machines have arrived, with 30 other boxes and barrels of gifts from America! As soon as they are released from Egyptian customs, we will receive them. It will be just like another Christmas for us!

We are now building a lovely building for the 1-to 2-year old babies. This building is being financed entirely with money which has been sent to us from the showing of the film, "The Nile Mother." We are naming this new building after the producers of the film, Mr. Harold Herman and Mr. Jan Sadlo. We will soon be ready to move into the "Herman-Sadlo Building." The workmen are busy plastering and the doors and windows are all in and waiting for paint. Of course the babies are all ready to move!

Just now our nursery of tiny infants has 51 babies. Their carriages are "bumper to bumper"!

March 1957

This year has indeed started well for us. On New Year's Eve a big truck drove up with a load of wonderful boxes and barrels from America. Brother McGlasson in New York saw to it that everything sent to the Assemblies of God warehouse in Brooklyn, designated for the Assiout Orphanage, was sent to us on a ship that left New York on November 26.

What a New Year's gift! I shall never be able to thank you enough or describe our joy as we opened barrel after barrel packed with the most lovely things our kind Christian friends could think of. There were boys' clothes, girls' clothes, baby clothes, quilts, towels, pictures, toys, and cuddly baby dolls. Most of the items were sent by WMC groups representing churches all over America.

We have the largest number of children in the orphanage that we have ever had at one time. On New Year's Day we had 1,035 — not counting any of the refugees who came during the war. Only a few of these have left. We may receive more orphans from Port Said; we have offered to take 25 or 30.

Our nursery is completely filled — 48 in one room. We just don't know what to do because, of course, we will never stop taking in babies no matter where we have to put them.

New children are coming in faster than ever before. The war has made it very hard for the poor all over the country, and poor relatives feel they can no longer support orphans. So they decide the best thing to do is to send them to the orphanage. During the last month we took in 28 children! Now we have 1,058.

I have just bought over a ton of cotton to make mattresses. We have enough blankets, as I bought 1,000 army blankets with money I was given in America. The WMC ladies and friends sent me a lovely lot of sheets. The trouble is, where can we put the beds!

Over 25 years ago a poor widow came to me with her four little boys. We took them in and educated them. All grew up and married. The oldest, Alfy, married one of my girls, and God gave them eight lovely children.

Last month I received a telegram that Alfy, who was employed in a government office in Cairo, had suddenly died of a heart attack. I rushed to Cairo for the funeral. It was indeed a very sad time. The children threw their arms around my neck, crying "Granny, Granny!" Poor little heart-broken family! Alfy had not been able to leave them anything; even the house rent was in arrears. So I start all over again — just where I began with them 25 years ago. They are indeed sad and broken, but their lives will go on the same, if not better.

October 1, 1957

How did it all start? When I was between 17 and 18 years old, I had a great desire to go back to my old hometown of

Brunswick, Georgia. I wanted to visit my very dear friends, the Judson Bunkleys, the family who first showed me the way of salvation. Finally, my mother agreed that I could go.

I was so thrilled with the thought of again seeing my very dear friends and the town which was to me the dearest place in the world. (We were living in Asheville, North Carolina, at the time.) I rushed off to the station long before train time. There was no one in the station except a sweet little lady, who also had come early. All of this was very important in God's definite plans for my life.

This little lady began to talk to me and asked me where I was going. I told her all about myself, and she in turn began to tell me about herself. She was Miss Mattie Perry and she had an orphanage in Marion, North Carolina. I was thrilled with her wonderful story. She had about 100 orphans in her institution! Oh, I was so eager to hear every word about it. She told me the work was run by faith. I had never in my life heard of such a thing — caring for and feeding 100 people and having no money in hand at all! She explained to me how God saw her needs and supplied them day by day.

I had always loved children, so I begged her to tell me all about the little orphans. Our time was short and the train came soon, but before we parted she had told me many things about her orphanage. It was called Elhanan Training Institute and had a very fine school and a special Bible course. Then she said, "Why don't you come to my orphanage and help me? At the same time you can study the Bible and continue your schoolwork." Before the train came I promised her I would think it over after I returned from Brunswick.

It was not long after my return from the South that I decided to go to Marion, North Carolina, to Miss Perry's orphanage. It was indeed a strange new life for me. I took a girl friend with me from Asheville, Miss Mary Freeman, a dear good Christian. But she did not like Elhanan, so she returned to Asheville after a short time.

I was very homesick myself; I did not like the food and the

work was too hard for me. But nothing could have made me leave. I never could understand why people run away from a hard job. So, I stayed on there in Elhanan and learned all the things that have been so very useful to me in my own work in Egypt — how to cut out clothes, sew, cook, take care of newborn babies, teach and oversee large numbers of children, and how to do without!

I also learned there how to trust God for the needs of everyday life. I had no money at all and no one sent me any. Neither did I write to people of my needs (which were indeed many). When my shoes wore out, Miss Perry had no money to buy me another pair. Well, someone sent in a box of old clothes and there was a pair of men's shoes in the box. They were not new, but they were better than what I had on, so I asked Miss Perry if I might have them. "Well, my dear, of course, but they are men's shoes." It took more than that to bother me. The lack of a pair of shoes was not going to make me leave or write home for money!

Many things happened to me from the time I met Miss Perry in the railroad station until I finally left for Egypt. I went 1 year to God's Bible School in Cincinnati, Ohio. I went to Dahlonega, Georgia, a college town, where I was pastor of a church. God blessed my efforts there very much indeed.

I traveled in evangelistic work in Kentucky with Reverend and Mrs. Sam Perry, Miss Mattie Perry's brother and sister-in-law, and I got a lot of very good training during those months.

In 1909 I went back to help Miss Mattie Perry with her orphanage. Some months before, I had met a young preacher who asked to marry me. I informed my relatives and friends of my approaching wedding which was to have been on June 18, 1910. About the first of June, a lady who had been a missionary in India came and spoke at Miss Perry's orphanage, telling of the great needs of India. For several years I had been praying that God would call me to the foreign field as a missionary, but it had not been God's time to call me. Perhaps He wanted to wait until I had entirely given up the idea and planned a different course for my life. Then He let me have the privilege of giving up all for Him.

While this lady was speaking, I suddenly felt the call of God! I have never doubted my call for one minute. It has perhaps been the one thing which has helped me very much in the times of great trials. I have always known that God put me here and that of course He would never leave me, but would always see me through everything. He has.

An altar call was made that night. I had been in the habit of going at once to help the seekers, but this time I fell at the altar myself and again gave my whole life to God to go wherever He wanted me to go.

After the service was over, I went to Miss Perry's bedroom and told her of my call. She looked at me, then slowly said, "Lillian, what of your wedding?"

I said, "I don't know, Sister Mattie."

Many letters were sent back and forth regarding the matter. My husband-to-be was a preacher and had a number of churches depending upon him. He felt he could not go where he was not called and leave the work which God had given him. And I could not fail my call. He suggested that I go for a year and he would wait for me. I said, "What could I do in a foreign country in a year's time?"

"One year? Two years? Three or even four years — I will wait," he said.

But I replied, "No, one can't do any kind of real work with a time limit." So after many tears, that was that!

December 31, 1957

Yesterday was a day long, long to be remembered by all of us. Nineteen very large boxes and drums arrived from America. All day long we worked undoing box after box, counting and sorting some of the most wonderful gifts the orphanage has ever had. Words cannot express the wonderful gifts our friends in America have sent us — all of the things which we need so badly, and they came just in time.

Today, New Year's Eve, we have 1,151 in the orphanage. We have been sewing for months (ever since August) to try to get enough clothes made for the children. To meet our needs we have to have thousands of articles! You folks know how much sewing you have to do to keep five or six little children with enough changes to keep them warm and comfortable. We keep several shoemakers busy the whole year round trying to keep us in shoes. Oh, wasn't I delighted to see all of those shoes among the clothes!

What a day Christmas is with us! The boys and girls were all fixed up when the Rotary Club of Assiout started driving up in their big cars loaded with candy, oranges, hundreds of yards of lovely cloth, large sacks of rice, and soap.

All day long people come from far and wide to give their large and small gifts. School children are brought by the hundreds to see the orphanage children. Strong men go in the nursery and come out crying! It is a sight one cannot imagine — 45 infants who have lost their mothers, playing quietly or taking their bottles, not on a loving mother's lap but with the bottles propped up against their pillows. But our babies are really happy; people seldom hear them cry. They are never left alone day or night. The girls in charge love them like their own children. Each girl has six tiny babies to care for. They make the formula and boil the bottles, and the widows do the washing. A new set of girls come on for night duty.

I forgot to mention all of the nice baby clothes and baby quilts which came in your packages; they are really lovely.

Just as I was writing this, I got a long distance telephone call from Cairo from a friend who told me to send someone to meet the 2 o'clock train; he is sending cheese and jam for the children's New Year's dinner. He already sent a large supply of macaroni and toys for the whole orphanage a few days ago.

Isn't it lovely to see how people from all over do such loving things to make my little children comfortable and happy! Who would have thought of jam? I am quite sure that hundreds of them never have had a piece of bread and jam!

It will take us days to properly sort all of your lovely gifts. Such gifts are more like a dream than real truth. It brings to my memory those old days when we used to bathe half of the children, wash the clothes, and wait for them to dry before we could bathe the other half.

February 10, 1958 — The 47th Anniversary of the Assiout Orphanage.

Many years ago I was sitting at my supper table just like any other evening. I had only been in Egypt 3 months. There was a knock at the door just like any other knock, at least I thought so. How could I know that with that knock all of my life would be changed and the lives of thousands of others?

It was a call for prayer — a very poor woman was dying and had asked for a missionary to come pray. I jumped up and said I would go. Mrs. Van Guisling also got up and said she would go with me. Neither of us knew Arabic, so Mr. Ghali Hanna said he would go, too.

We found a dying woman lying on the floor. I didn't see any furniture at all in the room, not even a table. A neighbor was holding a little 3-month-old baby trying to feed it from a bottle made of tin! It seemed that the bottle had been in use for some time, perhaps ever since the mother had been too ill to feed the baby, for the milk had become caked and green. Yet, the child was trying to drink. I had never seen such a sight in my life — the darkness of the room, the suffering, the lack of just everything! Oh, how awful to live and die like that! I had never known there was a home like that in all the world. You see I was very young and had only just arrived from beautiful America; I had no idea of the suffering of others.

I was soon to learn that and many other things. They gave me the baby when the mother died. I took her to the mission with me. The ladies all quickly started cutting and making clothes so I could bathe the child. She was about 3 months old. I am quite sure she had never had a bath. It seemed that no one had ever thought the child would need to change her clothes, as there were no buttons. Instead of having buttons, the clothes were all tightly sewn on.

We finally got soap and hot water and a pair of scissors and cut the stiff, smelly, filthy clothes off the poor little thing. The smell was so awful that it took days before she smelled normal.

Everyone was delighted until the baby began to cry all night long. This went on for several nights, then trouble started. "We want to sleep; we came out here as missionaries. How can we work if we are kept awake all night? Take the baby back."

"Back where?" Yes, God uses the small, weak things in life to do great things. If the baby had not cried for hours and hours at night, she might have grown up as the pet of the mission station. But she did cry and cry, and God was in that weak cry.

There was nothing to do but to take the baby out of the mission; it was true that no one could sleep. So the baby just had to go, but I was going with her. This was a new development; NO one agreed to this. Who ever heard of a young girl just out from America starting an orphanage against the advice of *everyone?*

But still the baby had to go. "Where?" No one could answer that. My sister, who came out to Egypt to see me settled, said if I left of course she would go with me. But very definitely she was not opening an orphanage. I said I understood that perfectly. Against the advice of everyone, the weak cry of a little baby caused me to walk out with $60 in my pocket and rent a house for $12.50 a month and furnish it with the rest of the money. I opened the Assiout Orphanage 47 years ago today.

Mr. and Mrs. Van Guisling came to help us for a short time, then returned to America. My sister, all these years, has been coming back and forth to see me. She has now sold all her property in California and expects to spend the rest of her life with me, helping keep the babies clean!

My $60 was soon gone, but at last my first offering came in. A little telegraph boy gave me 35¢. God bless you for your offering which has, like the 35¢, filled the day's needs.

March 9, 1958

As I sat down to write you this morning and thank you for your gift, I was not seeing your money at all. All I could see was a very strong rope drawing a ship loaded with children. This rope was made up of thousands of little weak threads and fibers all twisted and woven together, some long and some short, some weak and some strong. Not one of these weak fibers could move such a large, heavy ship as it crosses the dark sea of life, but all the threads together are safely taking hundreds of helpless ones safely to adulthood! Christ is at the head, safely holding the rope. While He lets us sit among the children and do what we can to make them safe and happy, we must always remember we could never guide this great ship without Him. If we ever get to the place where we think we can do it, that is when we will be floundering on the rocks.

Last year we started off with $390.91 in our account. The year is now in the past, our family has had enough of every thing, and at the end of the year there was plenty left over! Our total expenses for 1957 were $72,093.79.

I wonder if you can imagine how I felt one day during the last week in December when I found two babies in our infant nursery with polio! I rushed them to the American Hospital and the doctors there confirmed my fears. Then on New Year's Eve, while I was unpacking all of the boxes of gifts from America, two more were struck with polio. My babies!

Well, there was just nothing I could do but look to God. All day I kept repeating verse 10 in the 91st Psalm, "Neither shall any plague come nigh thy dwelling." We thank God that it is now about the middle of March and there are no new cases. Two of the children have returned from the hospital. The other, a very weak little baby whose mother died with tuberculosis, came home from the hospital after she got well from the polio, but she never got her strength back. She died last week. I wrote to Cairo trying to get some polio injections, but was not able to get even one. Then one morning a long distance call from Cairo from Mr. Pieton of C.A.R.E., asking me if I could use some polio injections. I asked him how he had heard of our need. He had not heard about it at all! He sent a young man especially from Cairo with enough injections for 225 children. He brought them all packed in dry ice and gave the injections at once. Never before have I been offered any polio injections!

April 9, 1958

I wish I were able to give you some wonderful reports to encourage you, but our work is so different from most works. It takes a lifetime for one of my babies to grow up and become important, if ever! But I know that someday they will be part of the men and women of Egypt who will carry the lessons and examples which I have been teaching them. Books may be destroyed, papers may be burned or lost, but seeds planted in the heart of a child may lie dormant for years and then suddenly spring into life. The child may have forgotten who planted the seed — names, places, and people — but these are not forgotten by God.

Sometimes I get my eyes on results, especially when I read of all those wonderful meetings where thousands are saved and brought to God. Then I begin to wonder if all of the "glory" really belongs to the preacher. Perhaps a little child many years ago sat at his old grandmother's knees and in the little heart a seed was planted which began to sprout and grow. Anyway our job is planting, and it is God who will give the increase.

Talking about babies, I believe we have the friendliest little babies in the world. They see so many people every day who are very touched and automatically give out love and kindness to them. And the babies who have always had love from everybody just return the love to everyone who comes along. Our babies don't meet a "stranger." There are more than 40 babies in the infant nursery.

The word for company is *duiff.* The children hear this so

much that a little boy about 5 years old was looking at a picture of a crowd of people in a magazine and showed me the paper, saying, "See Mamma, *duiff.*" Crowds are not crowds but friendly visitors or *"duiff."*

May 5, 1958

May God remember all that you are doing to help me raise these little ones whom He has sent to me for a home and a chance.

A chance? Yes, all they ask for is just a chance to be like other little children with freedom from hunger, loneliness and fear of tomorrow. A chance to be warm, have friends, get an education and have a home — a home where they know they are wanted and welcome. All of my children are getting this. Here they are taught how to live, how to die, how to be ready to meet life, and how to prepare for eternity. We are really trying our very best to give them the *lasting* things.

Of course, with over 1,100, we cannot give them all of the lovely little things which are provided in a private home for a family of five or six. But still I am quite sure that our children are really happy and feel that theirs is not an "institutional life," but a real home life.

I often send you pictures of poor little children as they arrived in the orphanage and then pictures taken of them later after they have been here for some time. You can see the outward change, but remember the inner change is far greater than just getting fat and having a pretty dress. Their expression changes, their eyes are alive, they can laugh and smile now. If you have some of our old pictures, you will notice that all new children seem weak, do not hold up their heads, and have a sad look on their young faces. There is no happy baby smile on the face of the little "new child." Can you imagine anything more wonderful than to help the baby's smile to start growing from inside?

A friend was wondering, "How can you keep on staying here?" I have often wondered if I could live if I had to leave! So you see it is just how one looks at a thing. As long as God gives me strength to be a help to the "new child," I hope He will let me be here to do my part. There is nothing like it in the whole world. I am hoping that the Lord will open the way for a new worker to come out soon and help me.

In a few days we will be losing a lot of our older boys and girls. The boys will be finishing high school and a number of girls will be getting married. Yes, this causes quite a break in our home life, but it is not as hard with us as it must be for a small family. Our empty rooms and beds will soon be filled up again, and life at the orphanage will go on.

You will be glad to hear that C.A.R.E. has just sent us some very lovely gifts, 10 carpenter's kits, 4 shoemaker's kits, 6 recreation kits, 4 lovely new Singer sewing machines, and 7 boxes of things for our hospital.

A short time before these gifts arrived, the Egyptian government sent a very lovely gift of clothes; these packages had been sent from America for "relief." Everything was in the very best condition and included items which we needed very badly indeed.

August 9, 1958

I get a real blessing when I read about how God had His prophet Samuel order a meal to be prepared and cooked for Saul, before he knew that God had chosen him to be king (1 Samuel 9:23-24).

Through the kindness of you and many other dear friends, God has provided the meals and all of our other needs.

You will be glad to hear that it has been possible for me to take a few weeks' holiday at the beach at my sister's home in Alexandria. I always take four or five of the children with me so they will be able to see the sea and the zoo and enjoy quite a different kind of life. So many of them have never been out of the Assiout District.

It is such a great pleasure for me to be able to take them around and show them the sights. Many of them have never ridden on a train or a street car. How they enjoyed their first ice cream, their first meal in a restaurant, their first sight of a big city lit up at night, all of the wonderful sights in the big department stores, and going up in the elevator or on the escalator. These are real thrills of a lifetime to our little girls.

They often say, "Mamma, we will never again have such a wonderful time." They will always remember seeing these wonderful sights and the smiles of the friendly crowds as they look at the old lady followed by a lot of excited little girls! Some stop and say, "Who are they?" I grin back and say, "Orphanage children." Their smiles become tender and understanding.

Once I took a newborn infant with me on an airplane. As I got off the stewardess said to me, "Whose baby is that? Where did you get it?"

I said, "From an orphanage; she is an orphan."

She took her from me and said, "Oh, the darling, did you get her from Miss Lillian's orphanage?!"

November 10, 1958

Our new school building is going up fast; we will soon be putting the ceiling on the first story and the carpenters are making the doors and windows. This new building will indeed make things so much more comfortable for the little boys and the teachers.

A few months ago I told you that a lady was coming out to help me. She is an American, Miss Rose Armenia. We are delighted to tell you that Miss Ruth Anderson also has arrived to help us. Ruth is the daughter of a missionary family, and strange to say she was born right here in Assiout!

I don't believe you folks can understand what it will mean to the orphanage to have these young ladies here to help me. There is so much which I have not been able to do for the children, first because I just don't have time to do all of the things that need doing, and next, at my age I just cannot do all of the overseeing that needs to be done. These young missionaries are now doing their best to teach our older girls how things should be done so they can teach the younger children. We certainly do thank God for their loving help. Pray for them. I know how different things are here from what they have left in beautiful America. But they both seem very happy indeed to have come.

What a difference schooling is making in the lives of all our children! I cannot imagine any better paying job than taking in a poor little child who would never be able to ever go to school, and giving him a chance. Our orphanage is the only one I know of where any number of such little children will find a free home and a free education, without which there is little hope of them developing into useful men and women. It is a very great responsibility that rests on the orphanage. If we do not take these children in, there are no other doors open to them. Their lives here are very simple, but perhaps that itself is the best part of our training!

1959

After 48 years in Egypt, I have found that the hardest days were the first days. Perhaps one wonders why. As I look back over the first 30 years of my work, it now begins to form a pattern. I was young, untried, full of zeal and energy, but I had not been tested. I first had to learn how to trust God for a stamp, a railway ticket, a suitcase, all such small things. As God met these simple needs, I began to grow in faith.

Larger and greater tests were put to me. I opened the orphanage. The third child I took in had bubonic plague, my orphanage was entirely closed, and I had to be carried to the hospital with a 106-degree fever. That could have ended the work, but it didn't.

I opened the orphanage again and started all over. He promised to give me double. Well, of course this promise has more than been fulfilled, but with many more trials and tests. Why? If I had not learned to trust God for the simple needs of a small orphanage, how could I trust Him for 100, 200, or 1,200 children and their needs? I just had to be taught the hard way, otherwise the orphanage would not have been a blessing today to young people.

Now that I am over 71, God sends all we need right here to the door. Of course, one would expect to hear that! Sometimes I feel that my letters may sound a bit too cheerful for young people going out to the mission field. Most people have not heard of our ups and downs, of the more than 30 years when we didn't have sufficient food at any one time for a week. Most of that time there was not a day's food in our stores. I believe young missionaries should hear both sides of the story, because the hard times will come first: a strange land, strange people, an unknown language, no money. And the missionary is unknown both in the country of their calling and in America.

I had no time for play. It was a very serious job I had undertaken. If one takes in a houseful of children, you can't drop them and decide you don't like the work. Perhaps that is one of the reasons God gives us the hard times first, so we can leave, if inclined to quit, and go back home before others are involved. But the Bible says, "Let no man take thy crown."

In looking over pages and pages of my dairy, I have picked out a few pieces which I found very real to life in those wonderful old days. Yes, those hard days were our best days. I was young and I saw that nothing was "too hard for God."

January 10, 1959

I am sorry to tell you that the two large shipments of clothes and toys which were shipped from our New York office (23 drums and boxes) were not cleared through the Egyptian customs in time to reach us for Christmas or even the Egyptian Christmas (January 7). We are hoping that they will soon be released; anyway, we do not have to pay customs on the things.

You will be glad to hear that this delay in no way spoiled the children's Christmas. They were provided with toys in a new way. Through the kindness of some ladies at the American

Embassy in Cairo, a large number of kind-hearted ladies and girls in Cairo and Maadi started working weeks before Christmas, making all kinds of lovely cloth dolls, animals, and bags with combs, pencils, and fancy pins.

After taking out their presents from the bags the children all lined up again to have their bags refilled with an orange, peanuts, and candy! We had some balls left from last year which were given out to the boys who were too big for the cloth animals.

The Assiout Rotary Club drove up in their big cars and the ladies had made hundreds of colored bags filled with candy. Also they brought thousands of oranges; each child got a bag of candy and an orange. So, on the whole, the orphanage had a wonderful Christmas!

But it was all too much for me this year. On the eve of the Egyptian Christmas, I was taken very ill. The doctors said it was because of strain and very high blood pressure, so I had to stay in bed all day Egyptian Christmas! I thank God I am better now, but still very weak. Please remember me in your prayers.

January 4, 1960

On this day my heart goes back 50 years to 1910. I was a young, happy girl of not quite 23, full of dreams of all the wonderful things I was sure life held for me. The most important of all was the 12 children I was hoping for. I wonder what I would have felt like had the curtain been lifted for just a few minutes and I could have seen myself this morning, 50 years later! Here I am — a tired, old gray-headed woman, looking out my window and seeing not 12 children but 1,200! I believe the shock would have been more than I could have stood. God, in His wisdom, softly draws the curtain of His love across the future of our lives and lets us live day by day.

What does it feel like to have lived and worked in Egypt for 50 years? It is indeed hard to describe, and I believe few have had a fuller life; with a family so large anything can happen! Each new day brings its joys and sorrows — full, happy days with plenty, and hard days with great needs.

So many years just slip by; some have faded out of my memory. We may have forgotten, but how very important a whole year was in the lives of our little children! We planted and watered seeds in the children's hearts, and what we did for the Lord and for the children will never be forgotten by the Lord.

The closing years are both joyful and very sad; it is wonderful to live long enough to see the results of your work but at the same time it is sad to look at my hundreds of little babies and young children and know someone else will have to finish the job.

I am planning to go to America this summer for the Sunday school convention and to visit my old friends, and I hope to make many more new friends. Springfield (our Assemblies of God headquarters) will arrange my itinerary. I trust that God will give me strength to take this long trip; it will indeed be a great joy to see you again.

November 1960

We have much to be thankful for during this month of Thanksgiving! Personally, the fact that I am back with my children again is something for which I can never thank God enough! No matter how wonderful America is or how wonderfully kind friends are to me, no place in all of the world is home to me now but right here with my children. Here, I am needed all day long. The children don't care if I am 73 years old! To them, time and age mean nothing, only that Mamma is back home again! Is there anything in the world more wonderful than being needed?

We just don't know where to put the new children as they come in; we have no place to put any new beds! Many of the children are sleeping three in a bed! (The beds are the proper size for one grown person.) You can understand what this means to the crowded children in the great heat of summer. You will be interested to hear what we have decided to do about this very important matter.

We have about 130 widows; most of them have young children with them. We have decided to construct a really large comfortable building for these young widows and their little children. Many widows come to us as soon as they lose their husbands. They have no possible way to support themselves and a large family of little children, so they come to us with a little bundle of old dirty clothes and a few loaves of bread for the children to eat. Those who come to me never have more than that when they arrive.

The youngest children stay with their mothers but the older boys go to the boys' building and the older girls to the girls'. The women do the washing, cooking, mending, housekeeping, bathing of the little boys, and making of beds.

December 12, 1960

It is so wonderful to see God's loving care for this work. As I grow older and less able to do the work which is so on my heart to do for the children, God sends in the finances we need from many sources.

I remember in the early years I would go in the storeroom and look at the hundreds of clean jackets, dresses, pants, and underclothes, then look at my hands and say, "I cut every one of those garments." Now, when I go in the storeroom I say, "The blessing is too great!" Ladies from all over America have not only cut but have sewn these lovely little jackets, dresses, and baby clothes. When there were 100 or 500, I was able to keep the girls busy sewing all the time, but now there are over 1,300. God knew I just couldn't go on doing it all. Of course, I still cut out the long pants and shirts for the boys. I just hate to entirely give up my old job.

I am no longer able to travel by donkey or boat to the villages, but I don't need to now; God has made new friends for us who send sufficient funds. Yes, it is indeed the hand of the Lord that is holding this orphanage. Thus has Isaiah 49:16 become a living truth in the orphanage — "Behold, I have graven thee upon the palms of my hands; and thy walls are continually before me." I sometimes wonder why any of us Christians worry, when He tells us our walls are continually before Him!

I have just received a letter from our New York shipping office telling me the wonderful news that a large shipment of WMC gifts of clothing and foodstuff was shipped on November 18, 1960 — 29 large boxes and barrels. But as I read down the list, I was made sad to see: "One fiber drum — sender unknown; one carton unknown; one carton buttons, sender unknown; eight cartons unknown." I only hope that somewhere in the barrels or boxes, I may find the names and addresses of these kind friends. My little girls help me address the envelopes by typewriter. One addressed it: "Address not given, U.S.A." I hope you won't get that kind of a "thank you" letter!

I am sending you a picture of the laying of the cornerstone of our new building for the widows. I believe ours is somewhat different from most cornerstones. Years ago, I got the idea that it would be rather wonderful that, if in the future the buildings should be destroyed, people digging in the ruins would find a glass jar with a Bible in it. So from that day to this, our "cornerstone" is the Word of God. We build our foundation on some part of the Bible, and there is no "stone" at all in our "cornerstone". But somehow it feels warm and loving that even the walls of our new building will continually be before Him.

March 10, 1961

February has passed but in passing it indeed brought up many memories, for it was February 10, 1911, when I opened the orphanage. A lifetime ago! Oh, how full the years have been. Little girls and boys have now grown to be old, gray-haired grandparents! New babies came to fill my heart with joy, only to be called up higher and leave me brokenhearted.

In those early days when we never had any ice, we had to

milk the cows three times a day to keep the milk fresh for the babies. One awful summer measles came with death in their tracks. Eighteen of my darling babies died! But still we kept on. The kind doctors of the town came to help me. They wrote the prescriptions for the proper medicines for the children, but we didn't even have money for food so we didn't get the medicine. God was very near in those days.

The little new girls and boys whom we took in during those dark days left us years ago and have their own families; they love to tell their children how God met the needs. Many of those wonderful answers to prayer were forgotten by me but not by them. Those times are a very important part of their childhood memories, never to be forgotten.

As the 10th of February drew near this year, I prayed that God would spare me that I might be able to give Him 50 full years of my life in Egypt. I was sick in the hospital on the actual day and my sister had been quite ill, but thank God we were able to be together. Some of the older boys drove my sister to the hospital and carried her upstairs to my room. Then I sent for a carload of little girls and boys whom I had raised since they were newborn babies. I filled them full of cakes until I do believe they for once had all of the cake they could eat. A very nice dinner was sent us from the orphanage; by that time my sister was a little tired so she went home with the babies.

The Egyptian papers wrote many nice things about the orphanage, which of course pleased me very much. In the afternoon many kind friends came bringing gifts and kind wishes. At last, tired and happy, I went to bed only to wake in the morning and thank God for having given my sister and me the chance to be together after 50 long years. I asked Him to let me raise a few more children before my part of the story closes.

Since then quite a number of very poor little children have been coming in. I may not be able to raise them until they are grown, but we will start them and the Lord will see that someone finishes the work.

June 9, 1961

I am very thankful that after quite a long illness and 11 weeks in the hospital I am home again in the orphanage and able to begin to do a little light work. Oh, it was very hard on me to see so much needing to be done while I was not able to do a single thing!

The Sixth World Pentecostal Conference was held in Jerusalem May 20-21. This was a very wonderful opportunity for many of our dear friends to come by and spend at least one night with us in the orphanage. Mrs. Marie Brown of New York, who has helped for many years, and many of the officials from Springfield have at last been able to see the work they have helped and encouraged since the early days of the Assemblies of God. Some of these important visitors have included Reverend Thomas F. Zimmerman, Reverend J. Philip Hogan, Mrs. Mildred Smuland, head of those wonderful ladies of the Women's Missionary Council who send so many clothes for the children, and Reverend Emil Balliet of San Diego, California. And there were many others who came who have long wanted to see the children for whom they have done so much. Many wept as they saw our children packed in our large church and heard them singing at the very top of their voices, so delighted were they to show the American visitors how loud they could sing. Who could help but be touched to hear these hundreds of babies singing the same tunes (with Arabic words) that the little American Sunday school children sing. And most of the children were dressed in American clothes sent by the WMC ladies in America.

On the Sunday I came home from the hospital I was very anxious to go to the service in our church. The church is a bit further than I felt able to walk so I asked one of my boys to drive me in the car to our church. Two babies who are hardly able to talk rushed up to me and one said, "Mamma, how are you?"

I said, "I'm better now, darling."

The other one looked up at me with love in his baby eyes and said, "Mamma, we are praying for you!" I feel the prayers and love of these little babies really give me strength to go on with my work.

Our new widows' home is progressing very rapidly. We are now building the third story and putting in lights and plumbing on the first and second floors. The foundation was laid last Thanksgiving. This large building will make the whole orphanage more comfortable. We have been very crowded for a long time, but we just could not turn away the new ones who came to us. So every room was packed until there was no place to put even one more bed.

July 2, 1961

As I sat in my garden this morning I listened to the many sounds of a "city" of 1,350 widows and children — babies playing, the laundry being carried to the widows to be washed, the water engines, the call of cows for their calves, and builders rushing back and forth with material on their backs for the new building.

Then I saw our big truck pull in with a load of cement and dump it, leaving a cloud of lime and dust. My mind jumped back to July 1911; my orphanage was then only 6 months old. It was so pretty with nice blue curtains around the babies' beds, a few pictures on the wall, a table and a few chairs, all of the nice things one could buy in those days with $60.

All of the missionaries said I could not do it! I had my first baby Leah, then John and Faheema, and now another little boy had arrived — Zackie. But Zackie was very ill. Never mind, I could take care of him. But he got deathly sick so I had to call a doctor. Oh, there was the end of my pretty little orphanage. Zackie had plague; the government stepped in!

All of my pretty curtains were jerked down and put in barrels of disinfectant, as well as all of my clothes. Zackie was taken to the pest house. (He is a great grandfather now.) Faheema and John got measles, which I was sure was plague also. Baby Leah and my sister didn't catch anything, but I collapsed and had to be carried to the American hospital with a fever of over 105.

But what about my orphanage? I would start again! Would I fail again? I had no money. Was God in it? What should I do? There was nothing I could do but read my Bible and pray.

As I look at the two world wars which He helped us to go through and at what He has given us — the very wonderful gifts of food from the American government and the lovely clothes sent by the WMC ladies, I really don't know how to thank God enough.

August 1961

I have been told that I have not raised enough preachers and that I have too many children. Who knows what God feels about this? It is He who will give the results of our labor, He who has followed every step of the orphanage for the past 50 years. It was He who said a cup of cold water given in His name shall not lose its reward (Matthew 10:42).

Perhaps you have heard of the life of a poor "unsuccessful" missionary who spent his whole life on the field and only saved one little boy. This little boy converted the whole island.

Last night as I was counting how many preachers the orphanage has turned out, I felt discouraged. I remembered flying over St. Louis, Missouri, one night and looking down on the wonderful, beautiful sight of thousands of pinpoints of lights which made St. Louis look like the garden of God. These were little lights, not big lights. Then I remembered my hundreds of little boys and girls who grew up from newborn infants and were fed and clothed on food given to us day by day (like Elijah's raven), who grew up, married, and lit little candles in small villages where they are now raising their children. What was taught them in those long ago years has been taught to their children and their grandchildren.

Perhaps God, when He looks down on Egypt some dark night, may see what you and I cannot see — weak little lights burning in the hundreds of villages all over Egypt. The light may be just a little home where some grown orphanage girl or boy lives, reading the Bible or telling some story of how God sent food at the very last minute.

Perhaps the candle shines no brighter in the village cottage than when such stories are told. And the eyes of little girls and boys shine with a new light and a new idea of a personal, friendly God who cares for their daily needs.

September 9, 1961

During this past year I have spent 11 weeks in the hospital. When summer comes to Assiout, it is very hot indeed, so all my friends felt I should go to my sister's home in Alexandria. I came in the middle of August and the trip was very hard on me. Upon arriving here, I had the worst attack I have ever had. I never thought I would survive the night.

Mrs. Lily Khayott, a dear friend, took me at once to her lovely home where I could get the very best care. The doctor spent the whole day with me. It was my heart and my liver. It is a strange feeling to see oneself slipping away from this life into another. Oh, but entering eternity is the part of it that seems so restful. Yet, when my mind turns to the children, the tears come. What will happen to all my children? Then I think, *The children are there in the orphanage. Surely they will be allowed to stay.*

I am very much in need of your prayers. I am better; I'm able to write this letter and walk around in my room. But I am still very, very weak. The orphanage is keeping the church open all day and the children are always praying, but we need your prayers very much as well.

October 8, 1961

Yes, over 50 years! Long ago on October 8, 1910, a young girl could not sleep. Would the dawn ever break? Would the great city of New York never awake? Sleep was impossible!

At last it was sunrise. New York awoke. Breakfast was ready.

But who could swallow it? Oh, at last I and my sister Jennie were leaving America. (I didn't know how dear America was then; one doesn't value things, does he, till they are gone?) The most exciting day in my life had arrived.

Brother and Sister Brown of Glad Tidings Assembly of God in Manhattan, New York, and a number of other friends all joined in the excitement as we rushed to the docks far too early.

Will I ever forget the deep voice of the great steamers as they prepared for departure? Oh, the thrill of it! Even in recent years as I passed the docks in New York, it all came back to me. A shout came from those on the shore as the ship shook and gradually moved away our past lives. I was off. . . off to a land I did not know, to mother children yet unborn, thousands of them.

My sister Jennie was going to see me settled, and then would return to America. Through the ensuing years she has been able to join me for eight or nine extended visits. Then in 1955 she came to stay permanently. It is a sweet gift of God that we can be once more together.

How wonderful that God does not let us see the future. If I'd been able to look ahead and see myself today with over 1,400 children to feed and care for, I'm afraid my heart would have failed. Now it seems to me a natural state of affairs!

On that long ago October 8, I never knew what a wonderful life God was going to give me. People used to say, "Poor Lillian, in that awful summer heat of Assiout with no money and all those children, spending her youth in the dirty villages. Oh, what she is missing!"

Poor dears, they don't know what they have missed. . .a chance to make over broken lives and to build up the most wonderful memories a girl can have of her youth. It wasn't just a matter of riding donkeys or spending sleepless nights because of the heat. There was the joy of repairing crushed lives, of loving dying babies back to life, of spending my youth for God. No, it was not a lost youth. Never! Now the memories are golden, priceless, and cannot be taken away.

December 1961

While writing this letter to you, I thought it would be interesting to ask the kindergarten what Christmas is. The answer came back in no uncertain terms, "Jesus' birthday." But along with the joy of celebrating this glorious birth, there will be many a whisper all month long of dolls, candy, and toys such as they have never seen before perhaps. The new children can hardly believe there will be two such wonderful days — the American Christmas and the Egyptian — and all the meat they can eat! There will be new dresses and new shoes, and many large cars drive up all day long bringing gifts and toys so that every child and widow will receive something.

But more than the peanuts, candy, oranges, and other gifts, it is the birthday of the Christ child! In lovely Christmas hymns, the children sing of His wondrous coming. No, our children will never, never forget their Christmases! I'm quite sure that none of you look forward to a bag of peanuts, an orange, an exchange of simple gifts, and the worship of the newborn Saviour with such a gleam of joy in your eyes as do our children.

Then to bring the birth closer, more real and alive to our children, at some time between the two Christmases our older boys and girls act out the story of the shepherds by night. There is the star over the manger, the inn which had no room for the Saviour, and the three wise men. We watch Mary and Joseph rushing to Egypt with the little newborn King. Some of our girls and boys have real talent in dramatics, and people in Assiout ask them to repeat their Christmas play in various churches. It is very realistic and I myself really enjoy it.

This Christmastide, our missionary, Miss Ruth Anderson, is to be married to a handsome Christian doctor, Habib Iskander. Dr. Habib has been caring for our sick children for many months, and has endeared himself to all the orphanage. We wish them a long, happy life.

Part Five:

The Orphanage Today

By GEORGE ASSAD
Director
Lillian Trasher Memorial Orphanage

More than 20 years ago Mamma Lillian went to be with the Lord but her message continues on and on. Our Lord has proven himself to be the same God Mamma Lillian knew, just as He was the God of Elisha after being the God of Elijah. He is still taking care of the many children who come to the home.

We now have 650 children: 80 babies in the nursery and kindergarten, ages from 1 day to 6 years; 208 primary boys and girls from 6 to 12 years; 160 boys and girls at the preparatory ages from 13 to 15; 112 boys and girls in high school and university; and 60 older boys and girls being trained to help at the home until they find jobs or get married. Also, we have 30 widows and blind ladies.

This big family lives within the one surrounding fence of the grounds on 12 acres of land. There are 13 main buildings which include dormitories, a beautiful church, the primary school building, dining room, bakery, storerooms, clinic, offices, water tower, and an electric engine. We have workshops for carpentry, sewing, and knitting, and swimming pools and playgrounds for recreation.

We were able to finish building a new nursery recently. Eighty children and staff are enjoying the wonderful and adequate building, which is composed of 2 floors, each with 4 wings; each wing has 10 to 15 beds, bathrooms, and a terrace. Each wing on the first floor has an air conditioner, and on the second floor we have fans. We have new washers and a dryer which we were able to get from the States. A hot water solar system provides a lot of water for the children's baths. We now have a new swimming pool and playground for these smaller children. This whole project stands as a monument which reminds us that God is still the same. He is worthy of our praise.

We are now moving by faith in building a new kitchen and repairing the dining room, which will cost $100,000. We thank God for friends who have always shared to make these essential needs possible.

Education in Egypt is becoming very important and essential for a better future. So after the children move from the primary school that we have inside the orphanage they are enrolled in preparatory schools in downtown Assiout. Then, according to their grades, they choose to study at trade, commercial, agricultural, vocational, or regular secondary schools. After this they are allowed to attend university.

For some who fail at school we have training centers that give them opportunity to learn skills and be useful in the home at the same time. This helps cover the needs that we have in sewing, knitting, needlework, and caring for babies — activities in which the girls are involved. The boys are trained at the carpenter shop to make all the beds, tables, and benches, even the doors and windows. The farm also must be cared for; we have 60 cows, 2,000 chickens, 50 pigs, 80 ducks, and other animals. Some boys are trained in taking care of the gardens we have around the buildings.

In addition to formal schooling the whole family is trained in self service; everyone has an assignment to do. Even the primary children are asked to help. During the summer and vacations the big boys and girls share in building, painting, and cleaning projects at the home.

The widows play a role in preparation of food, washing, and cleaning. The blind ladies are not exempt from making a contribution according to their health situation and abilities; one helps by translating in children's church and others help in preparation of food. It is like one big hive — everybody is doing something to complete the work at the home to which they belong.

Everyone also finds time for recreation. Playgrounds for basketball, volleyball, and handball are located in every section for the boys and girls. The boys are very fond of soccer, and the little ones have their swings. We have three swimming pools, one for the boys, one for the girls, and a little one for the kindergarten. These are a great blessing for the children during Assiout's hot summers. Our children have the opportunity for exchange visits with the YMCA in downtown Assiout. Some of our graduates who live in Assiout help with the recreational programs we always have for the children.

Most of all we put emphasis upon spiritual training and Christian education for our children; this is our number one concern. Four ordained pastors of the Assemblies of God of Egypt, who are graduates of the home, carry the responsibility of the children's spiritual welfare, along with staff members, Mobilization and Placement Service (MAPS) workers, and missionaries from the Assemblies of God of America. At this writing Missionary Dwight Dobson is the Assemblies of God representative to the orphanage, and Missionary Bernice Wheeler assists in day-to-day activities.

The spiritual program includes: worship services for all the family on Sunday morning; youth meetings twice a week; children's church for the small ones once a week; family altars in every section each evening before the children go to bed; church school on Fridays when school is out; vacation Bible school programs in the summer; and summer conferences, seminars, and Bible studies.

We follow a well-planned 3-year program for Sunday school, and we teach the children how to praise the Lord. We visit the churches often with our three choirs in order to be a blessing to those who bless the home. Some of our older ones get involved in outreach ministries during summer vacation.

I thank the Lord that I was brought to the home when I was 3 years old. I was privileged to have special training by Mamma in studying the English language. After I finished my primary schooling, I attended the American College downtown in Assiout where I completed my high school training.

At that time Brother Philip Crouch was the spiritual father for all of us as young people. He was the one who helped me personally in many ways. I wanted to serve the Lord from the age of 9. I was sure that my sins were forgiven and I found myself telling my friends at the home about Christ, with the gospel of Mark in my hand. I was always happy to share in Sunday school teaching. I had planned to attend the Presbyterian Seminary in Cairo but Mamma Lillian expressed her desire that I stay and help at the home, so I took some Bible studies by correspondence from America.

In the meantime I was also secretary at the office and had the responsibility of the boys' section, as well as translating for David Irwin who was then the Assemblies of God missionary at the home. I later completed my B.A. degree at Cairo University.

On October 15, 1959, I was ordained as pastor of the Assemblies of God church at the home by the laying on of hands of Mamma Lillian, T. F. Zimmerman, George Carmichael, David Irwin, and the Egyptian church board. More blessings were bestowed upon me, as the Lord had been preparing a certain young lady at the same time. Mamma Lillian wished very much to see us marry each other. This is Fathia, my wife, to whom I feel much credit should be given for working alongside me. We now have five wonderful children; two of them are helping already in Sunday school and vacation Bible school at the home. They also share in the young people's meeting.

I never will forget God's wonderful pouring of His Holy

Spirit in 1968 when over 200 older girls and boys were baptized in the Holy Spirit. This was just before we went to Beirut, Lebanon, to help with the Bible school and the outreach ministry. While in Lebanon I completed a master of divinity degree at the Near East School of Theology. We came back to the orphanage in October 1975, and I was asked to serve as director. We praise God for all His goodness and the times of preparation for His service.

I have spent most of my lifetime here, and I still cherish and esteem Mamma Lillian highly. The more I study her character the more I realize it was not Mamma in herself who was able to do these miracles or endure the sacrifices. Her faith in God was the major contributing force to the forming of her character. She recognized God's call on her life and had full trust in Him.

I have seen that Mamma Lillian looked always to God in hope. Day by day she lived to glorify Jesus — starting with simple and normal tasks that God gave her the opportunity to do. Her motto was always, "O God, since You enabled me to do the simple things that I could do, I have full trust in You to do the great things which I cannot do."

Mamma Lillian loved others and her love she bestowed on her children is still reflecting in their love to the younger ones — their brothers and sisters — at the home. And it continues on in an endless circle.

With faith, hope, and love a message can't die. The ministry of faith working by love continues on even though Mamma has gone to be with the Lord. We still serve the same God, and He never changes!

Our many friends today have the same faith and hope in God as well as a love for needy children. It is through your continuous prayers and contributions that we see God's work continuing day by day. We give praise to God and thanks to you all.

Assemblies of God
Child Care International

For many years the Assemblies of God has maintained flourishing child care ministries in several foreign countries. In addition to the orphanages in Egypt, Italy, India, and Latin America, we have other programs which provide one or more of the following basic needs for children: education, school uniforms, hot meals, and basic medical care. Some of the children in these programs have been left homeless by war; others have lost their parents through sickness or death; and in areas of famine or other disasters, some parents have no means of providing for their children. In most of our programs $15 a month will provide for one child, and in some cases it is possible to correspond with the sponsored child.

If you are interested in supporting one of these programs or sponsoring a child, we invite you to complete and mail the coupon.

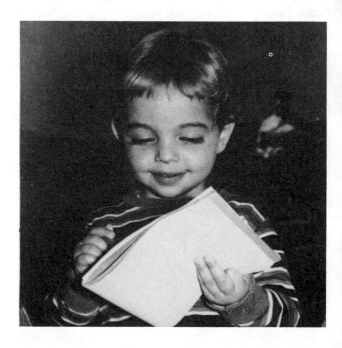

☐ Please send to me a copy of "Child Care International: Caring for Needy Children" — a 6-page brochure telling about the Division of Foreign Missions child care programs (order #71-7605).

☐ Please send me _____ copy(ies) of *Letters from Lillian* (order #71-7250). I am enclosing $5 for each book requested ($_____total).

☐ Please send to me information on sponsoring a child in:
☐ Egypt   ☐ India   ☐ Italy
☐ Latin American countries

☐ Enclosed is an offering of $ _____ for needy children.

Name _____

Address _____

City _____ State _____ Zip _____

Church to receive credit _____

Church address _____

Mail to: Assemblies of God
Division of Foreign Missions
1445 Boonville Avenue
Springfield, MO 65802

600-001 (521023) (00)   SC:GC